Praise f

Exploring Austi... with Kids

"This is an engaging, inspiring guide to Austin fun. Full of great ideas and hidden treasures. A boredom-buster that will inspire many family adventures."

—Kami Wilt, Founder, Austin Tinkering School

"So many entertaining and engaging opportunities!"

—Kelly Willis, Singer-Songwriter

"A fantastic resource for parents!"

—Staci Gray, Austin-based Children's Musician

"Lots of great tips are packed into this one handy book. It's definitely nice to have over 100 family-friendly outings laid out in one place, not to mention the fact that the entries are also cross-referenced by interest (think airplanes, sand play, and stargazing, for example), optimal age range, and location."

—Nicole Basham, Founder of LiveMom.com

"*Exploring Austin with Kids* is the kind of book I wish I'd thought to write (and had the chance to research!). It's fun, far-reaching and exceedingly helpful!"

—Liz Garton Scanlon, award-winning author of Caldecott Honor book *All the World*

"*Exploring Austin with Kids* is a go-to resource for parents who want to have family fun in Austin. Annette Lucksinger has clearly done her research, and provides a great service with this well-organized, comprehensive guide to kid-friendly fun in Austin."

—Jill Coody Smits, author of *Expedition Austin: A Kid's Guide to the Weirdest Town in Texas*

"I'm at that awkward stage of parenthood, with my children old enough to make and act on their own plans but with no grandkids just yet. *Exploring Austin* reminded me of places and activities I loved sharing with my kids when they were younger. Usefully organized from several perspectives, this is the guide I so often wished my family had, will happily recommend to ATX parents and out-of-towners alike, and expect to get plenty of use of myself."

—Chris Barton, author of New York Times bestselling *Shark vs. Train*, *Whoosh!*, *The Amazing Age of John Roy Lynch* and other children's books

"*Exploring Austin with Kids* is a fantastic resource. The information is up-to-date and helpful—for parents, grandparents, or anyone looking for kid-friendly activities in the Austin area. *Austin Family Magazine* gives this book a thumbs up."

—Kaye Kemper Lowak, Publisher of *Austin Family Magazine*

"*Exploring Austin with Kids* is just plain fun! Finally, we have a resource for families that explores every nook and cranny of Austin's nature scene and highlights its best-kept secrets. This comprehensive guide will help parents find their way in a city full of possibilities."

—Ryan Spencer, Director, Children in Nature Collaborative of Austin (CINCA)

"A fantastic guide for grandparents when planning those special days."

—Phil & Pamn Weaver, grandparents of three young Austinites

"Not only do I use *Exploring Austin with Kids* to plan my own family's adventures, I find the book invaluable as a teacher. It offers endless ideas that I share with my students' families to extend our science and social studies lessons outside of the school walls. It's also a great tool to plan exciting and relevant field trips as a class."

—Kelly Larson, mom of two and second grade teacher

"This wonderful book isn't just for parents! As a doting auntie with no kids of my own, I'm lost when it comes to planning outings with my niece and nephew. This fun, fresh guide saved the day! It's full of ideas, information, and inspiration for kids and the people who love them."

—Paige Britt, author of *Why Am I Me?* and *The Lost Track of Time*

"Annette's writing is a joy to read. It's not dry guidebook fare. She writes as a mom who is excited about checking out new places with her kids and her enthusiasm is contagious."

—Heidi Gollub, Founder of the blog Free Fun in Austin

EXPLORING AUSTIN with Kids

ANNETTE LUCKSINGER

Over **100** Fun Things to Do

Fourth Edition

Stomping Grounds PRESS

Published by Stomping Grounds Press
Austin, Texas

ISBN 978-0-9912270-4-4

Find us on the Internet at: www.ExploringAustinwithKids.com
For general inquiries: info@ExploringAustinwithKids.com

Edited by Annette Lucksinger with Jodi Egerton of Write Good Consulting and Laurie Filipelli of Mighty Writing
Cover and interior design by Monica Thomas for TLC Graphics, www.TLCGraphics.com

Royalty-free illustrations are from various contributors for Dreamstime.com.

COVER: City © Tasia12; Hand © Viola Di Pietro; Magnifying glass © Digiselector; Dinosaur © Petr Novotny; Food truck © Rceeh; Picture frame © Nataliashein **ICONS:** Bulb © Igor Dudáš; Slide © Andre Adams; Shoe © Ofchina; Purse © Anatolii Cojuhari; Food © Alevtina Karro; Globe © Dedmazay; Tree and bike © Notkoo2008; Flip flops © Elfivetrov; Van © Roberto Giovannini **INDEXES:** Kites © Oleksandr Melnyk; Map © Iryna Dobrovyns'ka; Airplane © Torky; Compass © Kytalpa; Tracks © Ievgen Soloviov; Piggy bank © Vladimir Yudin; Calendar © Natashasha **MAP:** Trees © Yuliia Brykova; Binoculars © Popcic; Restroom & picnic table © Candi4636; Hiking boot © Michael Mcdonald; Swimming mask © Rainledy.

Additional cover illustrations from Adobe Stock: Family SUP © TeraVector; Frost Bank Tower © iconsgraph; Crane © veekicl; Waves and SUP © lilkin.

Many illustrations were modified by Monica Thomas.

Fourth Edition

Printed in the United States of America

To Daniel, my rock,
Andrew, my adventurer,
and Stone, my homebody

Bucket List

These are the places I want to visit!

Memorabilia

Stick your admission stickers here, tape your ticket stubs,
draw a drawing or two to remember all the fun you have in Austin, Texas!

Table of Contents

FUN FOOD

Foreword

This project began nearly fifteen years ago when my youngest child, a homebody, decided to spend more time with Mom than at preschool. In preparation for the adventures we would have, I headed to my favorite bookstore to get a guide of the best kid-friendly places in Austin. I returned home empty-handed, having found little more than a few family-friendly pages in travel guides.

I saw a gap to be filled. With my son as my research partner, we set out to explore and document Austin's family scene. On the weekends, the whole family joined in — my oldest child, my husband, and even the dog.

During my four years of research, I experienced firsthand just how *much* Austin has to offer kids. I followed blogs, signed up for newsletters, and spoke with families about their favorite spots. My goal became to simplify these findings for others and make it easy for families to get out and enjoy time together. The result was a carefully curated guide that I hoped would capture the best of Austin for kids and prove a valuable resource to use with children of all ages and interests across the city.

As my kids have grown and changed since the first edition was published, so has Austin. Over the years, some of our favorite places have shut their doors. Yet at the same time, new openings of restaurants, shops, and trails continue to spark exciting, fresh adventures.

In revisiting each place to update this final edition, I found myself reflecting back on our family adventures — music concerts, camping trips, museum excursions, biking treks, and train rides. Exploring alongside my kids has filled this city with irreplaceable memories. I hope this book does the same for you.

Introduction

This guidebook highlights activities and events that appeal not only to kids of all ages but also to the fun-loving grownups that accompany them. Those new to parenting will find a guide into the entirely new city that appears with the birth of a first child. Experienced Austin parents will discover fresh places yet to be explored. Visitors will find it invaluable in leading to the must-see tourist destinations and the popular local haunts that make Austin such a vibrant city.

What's New in This Edition

Named one of the fastest growing cities in the nation, Austin keeps changing. While a few favorite places have closed their doors since the last edition of *Exploring Austin with Kids,* a slew of new ones have popped up all over the city. This fourth, updated edition includes those that continue to embody the Austin spirit to:

- Stay young at heart
- Get outdoors
- Support local enterprise
- Celebrate the arts, culture, and creativity
- Enjoy the unique, fun places that "Keep Austin Weird."

In this revised, updated edition, you will also find a few new things:

- new *Places to Eat*
- more *Places to Go*
- updated hours, admissions, and locations
- expanded day trips to *Surrounding Areas*

How to use this book

The Table of Contents arranges entries categorically by age, location, and activity type to help you identify outings best suited to your family. Pack the book in your backpack, stroller, or diaper bag for easy reference. You can use it not just as a guide to the best fun in Austin, but also as a keepsake. Tuck your tickets inside, decorate pages with admission stickers and photos, get autographs from the friends and family that you take along with you—or from the local musicians, performers, and authors you meet. Make it an adventure!

New Parents

On the day your first child is born, the city magically changes. Doors open to places you never considered visiting as you begin to look forward to trips to the zoo, movies surrounded by babies, and outdoor performances by children's musicians. The city becomes fun all over again.

To help ease your way into this child culture:

- See the "Baby" entries listed in the Table of Contents for good spots to get out with your baby.
- The "Places to Wander" section also offers suggestions for low-stress outings for parents and little ones to explore the world together.
- Later you can graduate to the "Toddler/Preschool" favorites. From there, your child's interests will likely influence the activities you choose and the places you go.

Experienced Austin Parents

If you are a parent with plenty of Austin experience under your belt, this book can lead you to yet unexplored places and make it simpler to visit those you have been wanting to see. Here are some tips for how to best use this guide:

- Toss it in the car or stroller and keep it there for easy reference as you head out to explore. Use the monthly *Annual Events Calendar* to keep you up to date on festivals and annual events. Make a family "to do" list and get going.
- On those days when boredom hits, when you can't decide where to go or what to do—pick a random page number, flip the book open, and head out!
- Explore someone else's backyard. Likely, you have a number of favorite haunts in a particular swath of the city, but try a new park, library, swimming hole, restaurant, or trail in a different part of town. Branching out a bit can be exciting as you discover the diversity of experience the city has to offer.

Visitors

In a fun-loving city that embraces the outdoors, live music, and local culture as Austin does, there is always much to see and do. Here are some suggestions to help make your visit a real success:

- In planning your trip to the capital city, be sure to check the "Top Tourist Destinations" in the Table of Contents that will direct your family to those uniquely Austin experiences.
- Each year Austin hosts numerous festivals that are fun for families, often several on any given weekend. Check the *Annual Events Calendar* for the dates that coincide with your visit.
- To truly experience the city, make time to explore any number of quirky places off the beaten path.

Icons

Look for these icons alongside each entry. They will give you a quick sense of the activities you can expect to find at each place. Cross-references are noted in bold, italicized font within the entries.

- Educational
- Active
- Cultural
- Entertainment
- Playground

- Shopping
- Food/Treats
- Museum
- Outdoors

Safety

Austin can get downright hot in the spring and summer months. So set out in the morning before things warm up and take care to guard young ones from the heat. It's always good to be prepared and keep an "emergency bag" stashed in the car for potential mishaps too, from bee stings or poison ivy to downpours and unplanned dips in the creek. Here are some ideas for filling it:

- Hats/baseball caps
- Water bottles
- Sunscreen
- Insect repellent
- Antibacterial hand sanitizer
- Picnic blanket
- Towel
- Spare clothes
- Rain gear/umbrellas
- Flashlight

Emergency snacks	Lighter
Pocketknife (or scissors/bottle opener)	Pen and paper

Petty cash (for unexpected parking, snacks, entrance fees)

First aid kit *(pre-packaged kits are available or put together your own)*:

Band-Aids	Tweezers
Gauze	Pain reliever
Disinfectant, hydrogen peroxide	Benadryl for allergic reactions
Triple antibiotic ointment	Hand cleansing wipes

General Advice

Call ahead

Each entry lists the most up-to-date information available at the time of publication. However, Austin is a dynamic city and things are constantly changing. So call ahead or refer to your destination's website to verify hours and admission fees before you go.

Stay on the trail

Poison ivy is prevalent in these parts. Stick to the trails when hiking to avoid wandering off into a patch of it. If exposed, wash the area with soap and water as soon as possible.

Check the weather report

Be sure to check the forecast since Texas weather can change abruptly.

Get buy-in

Kids will enjoy the experience even more when they are involved in the planning. Let them help decide on outings, map the route, pack snacks, give directions, and take pictures once you get to your destination.

Have fun

Get out and enjoy!

Categorical List of Entries

- A-Z List of Places to Go
- A-Z List of Places to Eat
- A-Z List of Annual Events
- Listings by Interest
- Listings by Age
- Listings by Location
- Free Activities and Events

Alphabetical List of Places to Go

Alamo Drafthouse

Ann and Roy Butler Hike and Bike Trail at Lady Bird Lake

Austin Aquarium

Austin Bouldering Project

Austin Duck Adventures

Austin Independent School District Playgrounds

Austin Nature and Science Center

Austin Public Libraries

Austin Rowing Club (formerly Congress Avenue Kayaks)

Austin Steam Train

Austin Zoo

Barton Creek Farmers' Market

Barton Creek Greenbelt

Barton Springs Pool

Bat Watching

Blanton Museum of Art

The Bob Bullock Texas State History Museum

Boggy Creek Farm

BookPeople

Butler Park

Camp Mabry

Capital MetroRail

Cathedral of Junk

Chaparral Ice Skating

City of Austin Parks

City of Austin Pools and Splash Pads

Commons Ford Ranch Metropolitan Park

The Contemporary Austin at Laguna Gloria

Crowe's Nest Farm

Deep Eddy Pool

Dinosaur Park

Dougherty Arts Center

Ella Wooten Pool at Mueller

Emma Long Metropolitan Park

George Washington Carver Museum and Cultural Center

Hamilton Pool Preserve

Hideout Theatre

Irving and Hazeline Smith Trail

Krause Springs

Lady Bird Johnson Wildflower Center
Long Center
Lou Neff Point
Mayfield Park and Preserve
McKinney Falls State Park
McKinney Roughs Nature Park
Mexic-Arte Museum
Millennium Youth Entertainment Complex
Mount Bonnell
Mueller Farmers' Market
Mueller Parks and Trails
Mueller Skate Park

The Natural Gardener
9th Street BMX
Northern Walnut Creek Trail
Pedernales Falls State Park
Peter Pan Mini-Golf
Pinballz
Pioneer Farms
Play for All Park
Playland Skate Center
River Place Nature Trail
Round Rock Express Baseball
Rowing Dock
St. Edward's Trail
Scottish Rite Children's Theater
South Congress
Southern Walnut Creek Trail
Splash! Exhibit
Terra Toys
Texas Memorial Museum
Texas State Capitol
Texas Union Underground
Thinkery
Tower Garden (aka Turtle Pond)
Toy Joy
Toybrary Austin
Turkey Creek Trail
Umlauf Sculpture Garden
University of Texas Star Party
University of Texas Tower Tour
Veloway
Walter E. Long Metropolitan Park at Decker Lake
Westcave Outdoor Discovery Center
Whole Earth Provision
Wild Basin Wilderness Preserve
ZACH Theatre

Zilker Park

- Austin Nature and Science Center
- Barton Springs Pool
- Lou Neff Point
- Rowing Dock
- Splash! Exhibit
- Umlauf Sculpture Garden
- Zilker Botanical Gardens
- Zilker Eagle
- Zilker Nature Preserve and Hiking Trails

- Zilker Park Boat Rentals
- Zilker Park Playscape

Alphabetical List of Places to Eat

Amy's Ice Creams
Big Top Candy Shop
Casey's New Orleans Snowballs
Central Market
Doc's Backyard
Easy Tiger
Flores Mexican Restaurant
Hat Creek Burger Company
Home Slice Pizza
Jester King Brewery
Kerbey Lane Café
Mandola's Italian Kitchen
Matt's El Rancho
Meanwhile Brewing Company
Phil's Ice House
Salt Lick
Sandy's Hamburgers
Ski Shores Cafe
Sno-Beach
Sugar Mama's Bakeshop
Waterloo Ice House
Whole Foods Rooftop

Alphabetical List of Annual Events

Austin City Limits Festival (ACL Fest)

Austin Dragon Boat Festival and Race

Austin Museum Day

Austin Symphony Orchestra's Tuneful Tales

Austin Trail of Lights

Beverly S. Sheffield Zilker Hillside Theater

Boo at the Zoo

Camp Mabry Living History Weekend

Christmas Lights on 37th Street

Crowe's Nest Farm Fall Family Fun Fest

Día de los Muertos Viva La Vida Fest

Eeyore's Birthday Party

Holiday Sing-Along and Downtown Stroll

HONK!TX Festival

Juggle Fest

Luminations at Lady Bird Johnson Wildflower Center

Nature Nights at Lady Bird Johnson Wildflower Center

Rock the Park

Rodeo Austin

Shakespeare in the Park

South by Southwest Festival (SXSW)

Squirrel Fest

Texas Book Festival

Touch-A-Truck

Waterloo Greenway Creek Show

Zilker Holiday Tree

Zilker Kite Festival

Listings by Interest

The symbol Ⓔ specifies that a listing is an annual event.

Airplanes

Camp Mabry

Animals

Austin Aquarium

Austin Nature and Science Center

Austin Zoo

Bat Watching

Boggy Creek Farm

Boo at the Zoo Ⓔ

Crowe's Nest Farm

Lou Neff Point

Mayfield Park and Preserve

The Natural Gardener

Nature Nights at Lady Bird Johnson Wildflower Center Ⓔ

Pioneer Farms

Rodeo Austin Ⓔ

Tower Garden

Arts

Austin City Limits Festival Ⓔ

Austin Symphony Orchestra's Tuneful Tales Ⓔ

Beverly S. Sheffield Zilker Hillside Theater in Zilker Park Ⓔ

Blanton Museum of Art

Cathedral of Junk

The Contemporary Austin at Laguna Gloria

Día de los Muertos Viva La Vida Fest Ⓔ

Dougherty Arts Center

Hideout Theatre

Honk!TX Festival Ⓔ

Long Center

Mexic-Arte Museum

Rock the Park Ⓔ

Scottish Rite Children's Theater

Shakespeare in the Park Ⓔ

Umlauf Sculpture Garden

Waterloo Greenway Creek Show Ⓔ

ZACH Theatre

Biking

Ann and Roy Butler Hike and Bike Trail at Lady Bird Lake

McKinney Falls State Park

Mueller Parks and Trails

Mueller Skate Park

9th Street BMX

Northern Walnut Creek Trail

Pedernales Falls State Park

Play for All Park

Southern Walnut Creek Trail

Veloway

Birds

Amy's Ice Creams Arboretum

Austin Nature and Science Center
Austin Zoo
Boggy Creek Farm
Central Market
Crowe's Nest Farm
Lou Neff Point
Mayfield Park and Preserve
Pedernales Falls State Park

Birthday Parties

Alamo Drafthouse
Austin Aquarium
Austin Bouldering Project
Austin Nature and Science Center
Austin Zoo
Chaparral Ice Skating
City of Austin Parks
Dinosaur Park
Emma Long Metropolitan Park
Hat Creek Burger Company
Lady Bird Johnson Wildflower Center
Meanwhile Brewing Company
Millennium Youth Entertainment Complex
Peter Pan Mini-Golf
Pinballz
Play for All Park
Playland Skate Center
Rowing Dock
Thinkery
Toybrary Austin

Boats

Austin Dragon Boat Festival E
Austin Duck Adventures
Austin Rowing Club
Bat Watching
Rowing Dock
Zilker Park Boat Rentals

Books

Austin Public Libraries
BookPeople
Terra Toys
Texas Book Festival E
Whole Earth Provision

Bowling

Millennium Youth Entertainment Complex
Texas Union Underground

Camping

Emma Long Metropolitan Park
Krause Springs
McKinney Falls State Park
Pedernales Falls State Park

Camps and Classes

Alamo Drafthouse
Austin Bouldering Project
Austin Nature and Science Center
Austin Zoo
Bookpeople
Chaparral Ice Skating

City of Austin Parks

City of Austin Pools

The Contemporary Austin at Laguna Gloria

Dougherty Arts School

George Washington Carver Museum and Cultural Center

Hideout Theatre

McKinney Roughs Nature Park

Scottish Rite Children's Theater

Thinkery

Toybrary Austin

ZACH Theatre

Creek Play

Barton Creek Greenbelt

City of Austin Parks

Irving and Hazeline Smith Trail

Lou Neff Point

McKinney Falls State Park

Northern Walnut Creek Trail

Pedernales Falls State Park

River Place Nature Trail

St. Edward's Trail

Turkey Creek Trail

Zilker Nature Preserve and Hiking Trails

Cultural Centers and Events

Austin Dragon Boat Festival E

Día de los Muertos Viva La Vida Fest E

George Washington Carver Museum and Cultural Center

Mexic-Arte Museum

Dinosaurs

Austin Nature and Science Center Dino Pit

Dinosaur Park

Texas Memorial Museum

Zilker Botanical Gardens Hartman Prehistoric Garden

Educational Centers and Events

Austin Nature and Science Center

The Bob Bullock Texas State History Museum

Camp Mabry

Crowe's Nest Farm

Dinosaur Park

George Washington Carver Museum and Cultural Center

Lady Bird Johnson Wildflower Center

Nature Nights at Lady Bird Johnson Wildflower Center E

Splash! Exhibit

Texas Memorial Museum

Thinkery

University of Texas Star Party

Wild Basin Wilderness Preserve

Farms

Boggy Creek Farm

Crowe's Nest Farm

Pioneer Farms

Farmers' Markets

Barton Creek Farmers' Market

Boggy Creek Farm

Mueller Farmers' Market

Field Trips

Austin Aquarium

Austin Duck Adventures

Austin Nature and Science Center

Austin Zoo

Blanton Museum of Art

The Bob Bullock Texas State History Museum

Camp Mabry

The Contemporary Austin at Laguna Gloria

Crowe's Nest Farm

Dinosaur Park

Long Center

Mexic-Arte Museum

Pioneer Farms

Texas Memorial Museum

Texas State Capitol

Thinkery

University of Texas Star Party

Westcave Outdoor Discovery Center

Wild Basin Wilderness Preserve

ZACH Theatre

Zilker Botanical Gardens

Zilker Park

Fishing

Camp Mabry

Emma Long Metropolitan Park

McKinney Falls State Park

Mueller Parks and Trails

Walter E. Long Metropolitan Park at Decker Lake

Hiking Trails *(see Nature Walks)*

History

Austin Duck Adventures

Austin Steam Train

The Bob Bullock Texas State History Museum

Camp Mabry

Camp Mabry Living History Weekend E

George Washington Carver Museum and Cultural Center

Pioneer Farms

Texas Memorial Museum

Texas State Capitol

Zilker Botanical Gardens Pioneer Settlement

Ice Skating

Chaparral Ice Skating

Live Children's Entertainment

Austin City Limits Festival—Austin Kiddie Limits E

Austin Public Libraries

Austin Symphony Orchestra's Tuneful Tales E

Beverly S. Sheffield Zilker Hillside Theater in Zilker Park E

Dougherty Arts Theater

Hideout Theater

Juggle Fest E

Long Center

Rodeo Austin E

Scottish Rite Children's Theater

Texas Book Festival E

Toybrary Austin

ZACH Theatre

Live Music

Austin City Limits Festival (ACL Fest) E

Austin Symphony Orchestra's Tuneful Tales E

Barton Creek Farmers' Market

Central Market

Día de los Muertos Viva La Vida Fest E

Doc's Backyard

Honk!TX Festival E

Long Center

Mueller Farmers' Market

Rock the Park E

Ski Shores Cafe

South by Southwest Festival E

Waterloo Greenway Creek Show E

Movies

Alamo Drafthouse

Austin Public Libraries

Bob Bullock Texas State History Museum IMAX and Texas Spirit Theaters

Long Center Movies on the Lawn E

Ski Shores Cafe

Museums

Blanton Museum of Art

Bob Bullock Texas State History Museum

Camp Mabry Texas Military Forces Museum

The Contemporary Austin at Laguna Gloria

George Washington Carver Museum and Cultural Center

Mexic-Arte Museum

Pioneer Farms

Texas Memorial Museum

Thinkery

Umlauf Sculpture Garden

Nature Walks

Austin Nature and Science Center
Barton Creek Greenbelt
Camp Mabry
Hamilton Pool Preserve
Irving and Hazeline Smith Trail
Lady Bird Johnson Wildflower Center
Mayfield Park and Preserve
McKinney Falls State Park
McKinney Roughs Nature Park
Mount Bonnell
Northern Walnut Creek Trail
Pedernales Falls State Park
River Place Nature Trail
St. Edward's Trail
Southern Walnut Creek Trail
Turkey Creek Trail
Westcave Outdoor Discovery Center
Wild Basin Wilderness Preserve
Zilker Nature Preserve and Hiking Trails

Parks

Butler Park
City of Austin Parks
Emma Long Metropolitan Park
Mayfield Park and Preserve
McKinney Falls State Park
McKinney Roughs Nature Park
Mueller Parks and Trails
Pedernales Falls State Park
Walter E. Long Metropolitan Park at Decker Lake
Zilker Park

Places to Wander

Austin Nature and Science Center
Butler Park
Camp Mabry
The Contemporary Austin at Laguna Gloria
Lady Bird Johnson Wildflower Center
Mayfield Park and Preserve
The Natural Gardener
Texas State Capitol
Umlauf Sculpture Garden
Zilker Botanical Gardens
Zilker Park

Playgrounds

Austin Independent School District Playgrounds
Central Market Playscape
City of Austin Parks
Doc's Backyard
Flores Mexican Restaurant
Hat Creek Burger Company
Mandola's Italian Kitchen
Meanwhile Brewing Company
Mueller Parks and Trails

Phil's Ice House/Amy's Ice Creams

Play for All Park

Salt Lick

Waterloo Ice House

Whole Foods Rooftop

Zilker Park Playscape

Restaurants

Central Market

Doc's Backyard

Easy Tiger

Flores Mexican Restaurant

Hat Creek Burger Compay

Home Slice Pizza

Jester King Brewery

Kerbey Lane Café

Mandola's Italian Kitchen

Matt's El Rancho

Meanwhile Brewing Company

Phil's Ice House

Play for All Park

Salt Lick

Sandy's Hamburgers

Ski Shores Cafe

Waterloo Ice House

Whole Foods Rooftop

Roller Skating

Millennium Youth Entertainment Complex

Playland Skate Center

Sand Play

Austin Nature and Science Center Dino Pit

Dinosaur Park

Emma Long Metropolitan Park

Play for All Park

Toybrary Austin

Zilker Park Playscape

Science

Austin Nature and Science Center

McKinney Roughs Nature Park

Nature Nights at Lady Bird Johnson Wildflower Center E

Splash! Exhibit

Texas Memorial Museum

Thinkery

University of Texas Star Party

Westcave Outdoor Discovery Center Star Party

Wild Basin Wilderness Preserve

Splash Pads

Butler Park

City of Austin Pools and Splash Pads

Sports

Austin Bouldering Project

Austin Rowing Club

Chaparral Ice Skating

Millennium Youth Entertainment Complex

Mueller Skate Park

9th Street BMX

Peter Pan Mini-Golf

Playland Skate Center

Round Rock Express

Rowing Dock

Texas Union Underground

Zilker Park Boat Rentals

Stargazing

Pedernales Falls State Park

University of Texas Star Party

Westcave Outdoor Discovery Center Star Party

Storytimes

Austin Public Libraries

The Bob Bullock Texas State History Museum

BookPeople

Thinkery

Swimming

Barton Creek Greenbelt

Barton Springs Pool

City of Austin Pools and Splash Pads

Deep Eddy Pool

Ella Wooten Pool at Mueller

Emma Long Metropolitan Park

Hamilton Pool Preserve

Krause Springs

McKinney Falls State Park

Pedernales Falls State Park

Walter E. Long Metropolitan Park at Decker Lake

Theater

Beverly S. Sheffield Zilker Hillside Theater in Zilker Park E

Dougherty Arts Theater

Hideout Theatre

Long Center

Scottish Rite Children's Theater

Shakespeare in the Park E

ZACH Theatre

Top Tourist Destinations

Austin Central Library

Austin Duck Adventures

Austin Nature and Science Center

Barton Springs Pool
Bat Watching
Boating on Lady Bird Lake
The Bob Bullock Texas State History Museum
South Congress
Texas State Capitol
Thinkery
Zilker Eagle
Zilker Park

Tours

Austin Duck Adventures
Austin Rowing Club
Bat Watching
McKinney Falls State Park
McKinney Roughs Nature Park
Texas State Capitol
University of Texas Tower Tour
Westcave Outdoor Discovery Center
Wild Basin Wilderness Preserve

Toys

Terra Toys
Toybrary Austin
Toy Joy
Whole Earth Provision

Trains

Austin Steam Train
Austin Zoo
Capital MetroRail
Zilker Eagle

Treats

Amy's Ice Creams
Big Top Candy Shop
Casey's New Orleans Snowballs
Sandy's Hamburgers
Sno-Beach
Sugar Mama's Bakeshop

Zilker Park

Ann and Roy Butler Hike and Bike Trail at Lady Bird Lake
Austin City Limits Festival E
Austin Nature and Science Center
Austin Trail of Lights E
Barton Springs Pool
Beverly S. Sheffield Zilker Hillside Theater E
Lou Neff Point
Rowing Dock
Splash! Exhibit
Umlauf Sculpture Garden
Zilker Botanical Gardens
Zilker Eagle
Zilker Holiday Tree E
Zilker Kite Festival E
Zilker Nature Preserve and Hiking Trails
Zilker Park Boat Rentals
Zilker Park Playscape

Zoos

Austin Aquarium
Austin Zoo

Listings by Age

Baby

Annual Events

Austin Dragon Boat Festival
Austin Trail of Lights
Christmas Lights on 37th Street
Texas Book Festival
Zilker Holiday Tree

Food & Drink

Amy's Ice Creams
Central Market—north location
Doc's Backyard
Easy Tiger
Flores Mexican Restaurant
Hat Creek Burger Company
Jester King Brewery
Kerbey Lane Cafe
Matt's El Rancho
Meanwhile Brewing Company
Phil's Ice House
Sandy's Hamburgers (drive-through)
Ski Shores Cafe
Waterloo Ice House
Whole Foods Rooftop

Outings

Alamo Drafthouse Tuesday Baby Days
Ann and Roy Butler Hike and Bike Trail at Lady Bird Lake
Austin Public Libraries and Baby Storytimes
Austin Zoo
Barton Creek Farmers' Market
Boggy Creek Farm

Central Market
City of Austin Parks
City of Austin Pools and Splash Pads
The Contemporary Austin at Laguna Gloria
Deep Eddy Pool
Ella Wooten Pool at Mueller
Mayfield Park and Preserve
Mueller Farmers' Market
Mueller Parks and Trails
Northern Walnut Creek Trail
Southern Walnut Creek Trail
Texas State Capitol Lawn

Thinkery

Toybrary Austin

Umlauf Sculpture Garden

Zilker Botanical Gardens

Zilker Eagle

Zilker Nature Preserve and Hiking Trails

Zilker Park

Zilker Park Playscape

Products

BookPeople

Terra Toys

Toybrary

Whole Earth Provision

Toddler/Preschooler

Annual Events

Austin Dragon Boat Festival

Austin Museum Day

Austin Symphony Orchestra's Tuneful Tales

Austin Trail of Lights

Boo at the Zoo

Camp Mabry Living History Weekend

Christmas Lights on 37th Street

Crowe's Nest Farm Fall Family Fun Fest

Día de los Muertos Viva La Vida Fest

Eeyore's Birthday Party

Holiday Sing-Along and Downtown Stroll

HONK!TX Festival

Juggle Fest

Luminations at Lady Bird Johnson Wildflower Center

Nature Nights at Lady Bird Johnson Wildflower Center

Rock the Park

Rodeo Austin

Squirrel Fest

Texas Book Festival

Touch-A-Truck

Waterloo Greenway Creek Show

Zilker Holiday Tree

Zilker Kite Festival

Food & Drink

Amy's Ice Creams

Big Top Candy Shop

Casey's New Orleans Snowballs

Central Market

Doc's Backyard

Easy Tiger

Flores Mexican Restaurant

Hat Creek Burger Company
Home Slice Pizza
Jester King Brewery
Kerbey Lane Café
Mandola's Italian Kitchen
Matt's El Rancho
Meanwhile Brewing Company
Phil's Ice House
Salt Lick
Sandy's Hamburgers
Ski Shores Cafe
Sno-Beach
Sugar Mama's Bakeshop
Waterloo Ice House
Whole Foods Rooftop

Fun Places to Shop

BookPeople
The Natural Gardener
Terra Toys
Thinkery
Toy Joy
Toybrary
Whole Earth Provision

Outings

Austin Aquarium
Austin Bouldering Project
Austin Independent School District Playgrounds
Austin Nature and Science Center
Austin Public Libraries
Austin Steam Train: Day Out with Thomas & Polar Express
Austin Zoo

Barton Creek Greenbelt
The Bob Bullock Texas State History Museum First Sundays
Boggy Creek Farm
Butler Park
Capital MetroRail
Cathedral of Junk
City of Austin Parks
City of Austin Pools and Splash Pads
Commons Ford Ranch Metropolitan Park
The Contemporary Austin at Laguna Gloria
Crowe's Nest Farm
Deep Eddy Pool
Dinosaur Park
Dougherty Arts Center
Ella Wooten Pool at Mueller
Emma Long Metropolitan Park

Hideout Theatre

Irving and Hazeline Smith Trail

Lady Bird Johnson Wildflower Center

Long Center

Lou Neff Point

Mayfield Park and Preserve

Mueller Farmers' Market

Mueller Parks and Trails

Northern Walnut Creek Trail

Play for All Park

Pioneer Farms

River Place Nature Trail

Scottish Rite Children's Theater

Southern Walnut Creek Trail

Splash! Exhibit

Texas Memorial Museum

Thinkery

Tower Garden

Toybrary Austin

Umlauf Sculpture Garden

Wild Basin Wilderness Preserve

ZACH Theatre

Zilker Botanical Gardens

Zilker Eagle

Zilker Nature Preserve and Hiking Trails

Zilker Park

Zilker Park Playscape

Grade School (ages 5-9)

Annual Events

Austin Dragon Boat Festival

Austin Museum Day

Austin Trail of Lights

Beverly S. Sheffield Zilker Hillside Theater

Boo at the Zoo

Camp Mabry Living History Weekend

Christmas Lights on 37th Street

Crowe's Nest Farm Fall Family Fun Fest

Día de los Muertos Viva La Vida Fest

Eeyore's Birthday Party

Holiday Sing-Along and Downtown Stroll

HONK!TX Festival

Juggle Fest

Luminations at Lady Bird Johnson Wildflower Center

Nature Nights at Lady Bird Johnson Wildflower Center

Rock the Park

Rodeo Austin

South by Southwest Festival

Squirrel Fest

Texas Book Festival

Touch-A-Truck

Waterloo Greenway Creek Show

Zilker Holiday Tree
Zilker Kite Festival

Food & Drink

Amy's Ice Creams
Big Top Candy Shop
Casey's New Orleans Snowballs
Central Market
Doc's Backyard
Easy Tiger
Flores Mexican Restaurant
Hat Creek Burger Company
Home Slice Pizza
Jester King Brewery
Kerbey Lane Café
Mandola's Italian Kitchen
Matt's El Rancho
Meanwhile Brewing Company
Phil's Ice House
Salt Lick
Sandy's Hamburgers
Ski Shores Cafe
Sno-Beach
Sugar Mama's Bakeshop
Waterloo Ice House
Whole Foods Rooftop

Fun Places to Shop

BookPeople
Terra Toys
Toy Joy
Whole Earth Provision

Outings

Alamo Drafthouse
Ann and Roy Butler Hike and Bike Trail
Austin Aquarium
Austin Bouldering Project
Austin Duck Adventures
Austin Independent School District Playgrounds
Austin Nature and Science Center
Austin Public Libraries
Austin Rowing Club
Austin Steam Train
Austin Zoo
Barton Creek Farmers' Market
Barton Creek Greenbelt
Barton Springs Pool
Bat Watching
The Bob Bullock Texas State History Museum
Boggy Creek Farm
Butler Park
Camp Mabry

Capital MetroRail
Cathedral of Junk
Chaparral Ice Skating
City of Austin Parks
City of Austin Pools and Splash Pads
Commons Ford Ranch Metropolitan Park
The Contemporary Austin at Laguna Gloria
Crowe's Nest Farm

Deep Eddy Pool
Dinosaur Park
Dougherty Arts Center
Ella Wooten Pool at Mueller
Emma Long Metropolitan Park
George Washington Carver Museum and Cultural Center
Hamilton Pool Preserve
Hideout Theatre
Irving and Hazeline Smith Trail
Krause Springs
Lady Bird Johnson Wildflower Center
Long Center
Lou Neff Point
Mayfield Park and Preserve
McKinney Falls State Park
McKinney Roughs Nature Park
Millennium Youth Entertainment Complex
Mount Bonnell
Mueller Farmers' Market
Mueller Parks and Trails
Mueller Skate Park
9th Street BMX
Northern Walnut Creek Trail
Pedernales Falls State Park
Peter Pan Mini-Golf
Pioneer Farms
Play for All Park
Playland Skate Center
River Place Nature Trail
Round Rock Express
Rowing Dock
St. Edward's Trail
Scottish Rite Children's Theater
Southern Walnut Creek Trail
Splash! Exhibit
Texas Memorial Museum
Texas State Capitol
Texas Union Underground
Thinkery
Tower Garden
Turkey Creek Trail
Umlauf Sculpture Garden

University of Texas Star Party

University of Texas Tower Tour

Veloway

Walter E. Long Metropolitan Park at Decker Lake

Westcave Outdoor Discovery Center

Wild Basin Wilderness Preserve

ZACH Theatre

Zilker Park

Zilker Botanical Gardens

Zilker Eagle

Zilker Nature Preserve and Hiking Trails

Zilker Park Boat Rentals

Zilker Park Playscape

Tween (ages 10-12)

Annual Events

Austin City Limits Festival (ACL Fest)

Austin Dragon Boat Festival

Austin Museum Day

Austin Trail of Lights

Beverly S. Sheffield Zilker Hillside Theater

Camp Mabry Living History Weekend

Christmas Lights on 37th Street

Crowe's Nest Farm Fall Family Fun Fest

Día de los Muertos Viva La Vida Fest

Eeyore's Birthday Party

Holiday Sing-Along and Downtown Stroll

HONK!TX Festival

Juggle Fest

Luminations at Lady Bird Johnson Wildflower Center

Nature Nights at Lady Bird Johnson Wildflower Center

Rock the Park

Rodeo Austin

Shakespeare in the Park

South by Southwest Festival

Texas Book Festival

Waterloo Greenway Creek Show

Zilker Holiday Tree

Zilker Kite Festival

Food & Drink

Amy's Ice Creams

Big Top Candy Shop

Casey's New Orleans Snowballs

Central Market

Doc's Backyard

Easy Tiger

Flores Mexican Restaurant

Hat Creek Burger Company

Home Slice Pizza

Jester King Brewery

Kerbey Lane Café

Mandola's Italian Kitchen

Matt's El Rancho

Meanwhile Brewing Company

Phil's Ice House

Salt Lick

Sandy's Hamburgers

Ski Shores Cafe

Sno-Beach

Sugar Mama's Bakeshop

Waterloo Ice House

Whole Foods Rooftop

Fun Places to Shop

BookPeople

South Congress

Toy Joy

Outings

Alamo Drafthouse

Ann and Roy Butler Hike and Bike Trail

Austin Bouldering Project

Austin Duck Adventures

Austin Public Libraries

Austin Rowing Club

Barton Creek Greenbelt

Barton Springs Pool

Bat Watching

Blanton Museum of Art

The Bob Bullock Texas State History Museum

Camp Mabry

Capital MetroRail

Cathedral of Junk

Chaparral Ice Skating

City of Austin Parks

City of Austin Pools and Splash Pads

Commons Ford Ranch Metropolitan Park

Deep Eddy

Emma Long Metropolitan Park

George Washington Carver Museum and Cultural Center

Hamilton Pool Preserve

Irving and Hazeline Smith Trail

Krause Springs

Lady Bird Johnson Wildflower Center

Long Center

McKinney Falls State Park

McKinney Roughs Nature Park

Mexic-Arte Museum
Millennium Youth Entertainment Complex
Mount Bonnell
Mueller Parks and Trails
Mueller Skate Park
9th Street BMX
Northern Walnut Creek Trail
Pedernales Falls State Park
Peter Pan Mini-Golf
Playland Skate Center
River Place Nature Trail
Round Rock Express
Rowing Dock
St. Edward's Trail
Southern Walnut Creek Trail
Texas Memorial Museum
Texas State Capitol
Texas Union Underground
Turkey Creek Trail
University of Texas Star Party
University of Texas Tower Tour
Veloway
Walter E. Long Metropolitan Park at Decker Lake

Westcave Outdoor Discovery Center
Wild Basin Wilderness Preserve
ZACH Theatre
Zilker Nature Preserve and Hiking Trails
Zilker Park Boat Rentals

Listings by Location

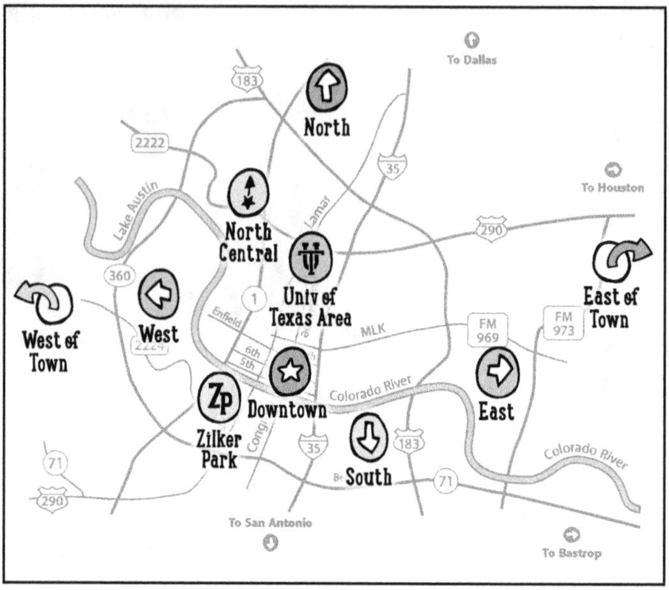

North

Alamo Drafthouse
Amy's Ice Creams
Austin Aquarium
Austin Independent School District Playgrounds
Austin Public Libraries
Austin Steam Train
Capital MetroRail
City of Austin Parks
City of Austin Pools and Splash Pads
Flores Mexican Restaurant
Hat Creek Burger Company
Kerbey Lane Café
Mandola's Italian Kitchen
Northern Walnut Creek Trail
Phil's Ice House
Pinballz
Pioneer Farms
Play for All Park
Round Rock Express Baseball

North Central

Alamo Drafthouse
Amy's Ice Creams
Austin Independent School District Playgrounds
Austin Public Libraries
Capital MetroRail

Casey's New Orleans Snowballs

Central Market

Chaparral Ice Skating

City of Austin Parks

City of Austin Pools and Splash Pads

Ella Wooten Pool at Mueller

Hat Creek Burger Company

Home Slice Pizza

Kerbey Lane Café

Mandola's Italian Kitchen

Mueller Farmers' Market

Mueller Parks and Trails

Mueller Skate Park

Phil's Ice House

Playland Skate Center

Sno-Beach

Terra Toys

Thinkery

Toy Joy

Toybrary Austin

University of Texas area

Amy's Ice Creams

Blanton Museum of Art

The Bob Bullock Texas State History Museum

City of Austin Parks

City of Austin Pools and Splash Pads

Kerbey Lane Café

Texas Memorial Museum

Texas Union Underground

Tower Garden

University of Texas Star Party

University of Texas Tower Tour

Downtown

Amy's Ice Creams

Ann and Roy Butler Hike and Bike Trail at Lady Bird Lake

Austin Duck Adventures

Austin Public Libraries

Austin Rowing Club

Bat Watching

BookPeople

Capital MetroRail

Hideout Theatre

Mexic-Arte Museum

9th Street BMX

Scottish Rite Children's Theater

Texas State Capitol

Toy Joy

Whole Earth Provision

Whole Foods Rooftop

West Austin

Amy's Ice Creams

Austin Independent School District Playgrounds

Austin Public Libraries

Barton Creek Farmers' Market

Barton Creek Greenbelt
Camp Mabry
City of Austin Parks
City of Austin Pools and Splash Pads
Commons Ford Ranch Metropolitan Park
The Contemporary Austin at Laguna Gloria
Deep Eddy Pool
Emma Long Metropolitan Park
Hat Creek Burger Company
Irving and Hazeline Smith Trail
Jester King Brewery
Kerbey Lane Café
Mayfield Park and Preserve
Mount Bonnell
The Natural Gardener
River Place Nature Trail
St. Edward's Trail
Ski Shores Cafe
Turkey Creek Trail
Waterloo Ice House
Wild Basin Wilderness Preserve

West of Town

Amy's Ice Creams
Austin Zoo
Flores Mexican Restaurant
Hamilton Pool Preserve
Hat Creek Burger Company
Krause Springs
Mandola's Italian Kitchen
Pedernales Falls State Park
Westcave Outdoor Discovery Center

East Austin

Amy's Ice Creams
Ann and Roy Butler Hike and Bike Trail at Lady Bird Lake
Austin Bouldering Project
Austin Independent School District Playgrounds
Austin Public Libraries
Boggy Creek Farm
Capital MetroRail
City of Austin Parks
City of Austin Pools and Splash Pads
George Washington Carver Museum and Cultural Center
Millennium Youth Entertainment Complex
Southern Walnut Creek Trail
Walter E. Long Metropolitan Park at Decker Lake

East of Town

Crowe's Nest Farm
Dinosaur Park
McKinney Falls State Park
McKinney Roughs Nature Park

South Austin

Alamo Drafthouse
Amy's Ice Creams
Austin Bouldering Project
Austin Independent School District Playgrounds
Austin Public Libraries
Barton Creek Greenbelt
Big Top Candy Shop
Butler Park
Cathedral of Junk
City of Austin Parks
City of Austin Pools and Splash Pads
Doc's Backyard
Dougherty Arts Center
Easy Tiger
Flores Mexican Restaurant
Home Slice Pizza
Kerbey Lane Café
Lady Bird Johnson Wildflower Center
Long Center
Mandola's Italian Kitchen
Matt's El Rancho
Meanwhile Brewing Company
Peter Pan Mini-Golf
Phil's Ice House
Salt Lick
Sandy's Hamburgers
Sno-Beach
South Congress
Sugar Mama's Bakeshop
Veloway
Waterloo Ice House
Whole Earth Provision
ZACH Theatre

Zilker Park

Ann and Roy Butler Hike and Bike Trail at Lady Bird Lake
Austin Nature and Science Center
Barton Creek Greenbelt
Barton Springs Pool
Lou Neff Point
Rowing Dock
Splash! Exhibit
Umlauf Sculpture Garden
Zilker Botanical Gardens
Zilker Eagle
Zilker Nature Preserve and Hiking Trails
Zilker Park Boat Rentals
Zilker Park Playscape

Free Activities and Events

Free Places

- Ann and Roy Butler Hike and Bike Trail at Lady Bird Lake
- Austin Independent School District Playgrounds
- Austin Public Libraries
- Barton Creek Farmers' Market
- Barton Creek Greenbelt
- Bat Watching
- Boggy Creek Farm
- Butler Park
- Camp Mabry
- City of Austin Parks
- City of Austin Neighborhood Pools and Splash Pads
- Commons Ford Ranch Metropolitan Park
- George Washington Carver Museum and Cultural Center
- Irving and Hazeline Smith Trail
- Mayfield Park and Preserve
- Mount Bonnell
- Mueller Farmers' Market
- Mueller Parks and Trails
- Mueller Skate Park
- 9th Street BMX
- Northern Walnut Creek Trail
- Play for All Park
- St. Edward's Trail

- South Congress
- Southern Walnut Creek Trail
- Texas State Capitol
- Tower Garden
- Turkey Creek Trail
- University of Texas Star Party
- Veloway
- Zilker Park
  - Austin Nature and Science Center
  - Lou Neff Point
  - Splash! Exhibit
  - Zilker Nature Preserve and Hiking Trails
  - Zilker Park Playscape

Occasionally Free

Blanton Museum of Art: Free admission Tuesdays

Bob Bullock Texas State History Museum: First Sundays 10AM–5PM

The Contemporary Austin at Laguna Gloria: Free admission Thursdays

Long Center: Free Fun Family Events

Mexic-Arte Museum: Free admission Sundays

Thinkery
Community Nights by donation Tuesdays 3PM–7PM and Sundays 3PM–5PM

Umlauf Sculpture Museum: Free Second Sundays

Free Annual Events

Austin Dragon Boat Festival

Austin Museum Day

Austin Symphony Orchestra's Tuneful Tales

Austin Trail of Lights (select nights)

Beverly S. Sheffield Zilker Hillside Theater

Camp Mabry Living History Weekend

Christmas Lights on 37th Street

Día de los Muertos Viva La Vida Fest

Eeyore's Birthday Party

Holiday Sing-Along and Downtown Stroll

HONK!TX Festival

Nature Nights at Lady Bird Wildflower Center

Rock the Park

Shakespeare in the Park

Squirrel Fest

Texas Book Festival

Waterloo Greenway Creek Show

Zilker Holiday Tree

Zilker Kite Festival

Places to Go

The city's best local, outdoorsy, cultural and "weird" family-friendly places

Alamo Drafthouse

Be warned: watching a movie at the Alamo Drafthouse will spoil you and make any other movie theater pale in comparison. In addition to popcorn (with real melted butter) and bottomless sodas, the theater features a full menu ranging from classic cheese pizzas, burgers, and milkshakes on the kids' menu to the likes of Hatch green chili queso, fried chicken sandwiches with Asian slaw, or brisket burgers for adults. Wine, beer, movie-themed drink concoctions, and dessert selections are also available. While movie candy is always an option, so are adult milkshakes, root beer floats, or freshly baked cookies.

Place your order on cards that servers sneak by to collect. Then dine at the tabletop in front of you and watch the show. Arrive early for a real treat: the short films and animated classics dug up from the archives and thematically tied to the feature presentation. The Alamo Drafthouse's signature events are also perfect for date nights, from quote-alongs to dinner and drink specials uniquely paired with the featured film.

With plenty of expertise and attitude, the Alamo Drafthouse takes the movie experience seriously. So texting, talking, or children under six (except during kid events and weekly sensory-friendly screenings) are not allowed. That said, they also have quite a bit of fun with the whole movie-going affair and cater to young crowds during special events such as these:

Alamo for All—Infants or children with sensory sensitivities and their parents are welcome to special screenings on select showings when the sound is slightly lowered and house lights are slightly brightened. If infants fuss a bit, you'll find yourself among a tolerant crowd, and no one will kick them out. Free for babies.

Alamo Kids' Camp—The Alamo hosts several affordable movies at locations around town during school breaks and the hot summer months. The online calendar lists showings, times, and locations as well as special screenings of children's classics throughout the year.

Multiple Locations

LOCATION & PHONE

North

Lakeline
14028 N US Hwy. 183, Bldg. F
(512) 861-7070

North Central

The Village
2700 W. Anderson Ln.
(512) 861-7030

Mueller
1911 Aldrich St., Ste. 120
(512) 572-1425

South

South Lamar
1120 S. Lamar Blvd.
(512) 861-7040

Slaughter Lane
5701 W. Slaughter Ln.
(512) 861-7060

WEBSITE www.drafthouse.com/austin

Ann and Roy Butler Hike and Bike Trail at Lady Bird Lake

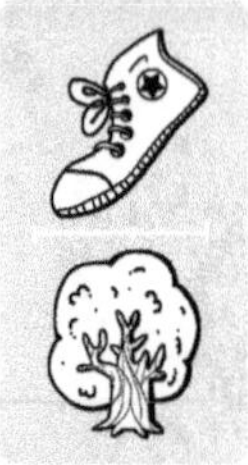

Jogging and Walking

This highly popular trail among joggers, bikers, and walkers runs 10 miles through the heart of the city along Lady Bird Lake. It's a beautiful trail and the crushed gravel path makes it a good one for jogging strollers. Especially ideal for parents wanting to get out and exercise is the 4-mile loop from the Mopac bridge to South First Street. Depending on how long your little one is content in a stroller, this stretch can be easily turned into shorter or longer loops. (See interactive trail map.)

Biking

For biking with kids, try the Boardwalk and 6 miles of trail east of Congress Avenue. This section of the trail tends to be much less crowded, and the paved Boardwalk that stretches along the south side of the lake — and above it — makes for a fun, easy ride with plenty of pull-off spots to rest and look out to spot water birds, turtles sunning on logs, and views of the cityscape in the distance. If you start on the north side of the lake, pedal on crushed granite paths along shady Festival Beach. Then head east to cross Longhorn Dam, or for an easier trek, turn west towards downtown to pass sculptures, the Mexican American Cultural Center, and a steel bridge that takes you to Waller Creek Boathouse where you can stop at the café for a snack on the patio overlooking the water.

Easy Adventuring

If you'd like to take things a bit slower and just enjoy time outdoors together, there are plenty of opportunities to diverge from the trail for short excursions. (See ***Butler Park, Zilker Eagle***, and ***Zilker Playscape***.) For some lake action, head to ***Lou Neff Point*** to see the ducks. Pack a snack and rest at the gazebo with a clear view of downtown Austin across the water. Canoeing and kayaking are also popular activities along the trail. (See ***Zilker Park Boat Rentals*** and ***Austin Rowing Club***.)

Take a peek at the interactive map online for locations of restrooms, water fountains, and trail highlights.

South Austin

LOCATION The trail loops from below the Mopac Expy./ Loop 1 bridge on the west end to Longhorn Dam at Pleasant Valley Rd. to the east.

PARKING Several options, depending on where you would like to enter the trail. Listed from west to east:

Mopac bridge:
A large unpaved parking lot sits beneath the Mopac Expy./Loop 1 bridge at Stratford Dr.

Austin High School:
Street parking and an unpaved lot can be found along the stretch of trail in front of Austin High School (1715 W. Cesar Chavez St.).

Zilker Park:
The parking lot at 2000 Lou Neff Dr. lies just above the trail. Or enter across the street at 2100 Barton Springs Rd. and park near the Zilker Playscape. Stairs leading down to Barton Creek will put you on the trail. (Note that paid meter parking is in force on weekends.)

Riverside Drive near Auditorium Shores:
Street parking and a few small lots are available along W. Riverside Dr. (between S. 1st St. and Lamar Blvd.)

Festival Beach:
Parking lots are available along Festival Beach to the east of I-35 at 2101 Bergman St.

Lakeshore Blvd.:
Also a good spot to park and bike, street parking is available along S. Lakeshore Blvd. between Riverside Dr. and Pleasant Valley Rd.

TRAIL MAP www.thetrailconservancy.org

ADMISSION Free

Austin Aquarium

The Austin Aquarium differs from a traditional aquarium, offering guests plenty of surprises. Located in a shopping center, the space is larger than it appears on the outside and contains not only tanks of fish and sea life but exhibits filled with reptiles, birds, and bunnies, a small climbing playscape, a concession area, and a gift shop. In many ways, it feels like a mini-indoor zoo. In fact, upon entering, visitors are greeted by birds. Then turn the corner to search for lemurs and coatimundis or iguanas before entering a darker space made brilliant by colorful tanks of tropical fish, coral, seahorses, jellyfish, and octopi.

A favorite exhibit among many—a touch tank for stingrays—fills the next room and highlights one of the aquarium's main missions to promote education through interactive experiences with animal life. Staff walk through the aquarium sharing information or offering views of animals up close. Tokens can be purchased to feed the fish or to go on animal encounters.

Check the website for information on field trips, birthday parties, and special events.

North Austin

LOCATION	13530 N. Hwy. 183	
WEBSITE	www.austinaquarium.com	
PHONE	(512) 222-5586	
HOURS	Sunday–Thursday	10AM–7PM
	Friday–Saturday	10AM–8PM
ADMISSION	Free	children under 3 and educators
	$17.95	children
	$22.95	adults
	$20.95	seniors and military

Austin Bouldering Project

For active kids, Austin Bouldering Project provides a fun way to burn off energy. As you enter and head to the check-in desk, you can catch a glimpse of grey boulder-like structures dotted strategically with knobby holds of all sizes, shapes, and colors, looking like modern day art pieces or a child's playroom floor turned on its side. Throughout the building, bouldering sections are arranged by ability level—toddler to adult—with color-coded holds to represent level of difficulty. So climbers can easily find their comfort zone or push themselves. All the climbing floors are padded.

Austin Bouldering Project has two locations. Towards the back of each, youth climbing walls present a range of challenges, from easy to more difficult. Another toddler wall offers the added climbing incentive of reaching hidden tunnels within the play structure. After young climbers get some practice under their belts, they are welcome (under close adult supervision) in the spacious adult climbing areas.

Passionate about bouldering and bringing the sport to others, ABP staff lead after school clubs, summer camps, parents' night out events, birthday parties, and personal or group lessons.

Want to add ropes? Check out Crux Climbing Center, another kid-friendly option.

Multiple Locations

LOCATION, PHONE, AND HOURS

East Austin

Springdale
979 Springdale Rd.
(512) 645-4633

South

Westgate
4477 S. Lamar Blvd.
(737) 237-0899

WEBSITE	www.austinboulderingproject.com
HOURS	Monday – Friday 6AM – 11PM Saturday – Sunday 8AM – 10PM
ADMISSION	$13 youth day pass (ages 13 and under) $18 young adult day pass (ages 14 – 23) $20 adult day pass Free shoe rentals for first-time visitors. Subsequent rentals are $4. 10-punch passes plus individual and family memberships available.

Austin Duck Adventures

Visitors will enjoy this open-air tour of the city in an amphibious vehicle that travels from downtown *into* Lake Austin. Locals will likely learn some new nuggets of information as well. For instance, did you know that ***Deep Eddy*** is the oldest public pool in the state of Texas, and that City Hall was built in the shape of an armadillo? The tour covers historic downtown buildings, the Capitol and Governor's Mansion, then heads west down Sixth Street to Lake Austin Boulevard. Children are kept busy quacking with souvenir duckbills and waving to passersby while anticipating the big *splash* into Lake Austin where they get an up-close view of the Tom Miller dam. The entire tour lasts approximately one hour and fifteen minutes. Drinks are allowed on board and restrooms are available at the Austin Visitor Center, the pick-up and drop-off point for the duck boat. Reservations are recommended.

Downtown Austin

LOCATION Tours begin from the Austin Visitor Center located at 602 E. 4th St.

PARKING Austin Convention Center Garage or curbside metered parking is available.

WEBSITE www.austinducks.com

PHONE (512) 477-5274

HOURS To ensure your reservation, arrive fifteen to thirty minutes early.

Summer hours (June 1 – Labor Day):

Monday – Friday	10AM, noon, 2PM
Saturday	10AM, noon, 2PM, 4PM
Sunday	11AM, 1PM, 3PM

Regular hours:

Monday – Tuesday	2PM
Wednesday – Friday	11AM, 2PM
Saturday – Sunday	11AM, 1PM, 3PM

Places to Go

ADMISSION	Free	children 2 and under
	$25.50	children ages 3-12
	$39.50	adults
	$36.50	students, seniors, military

Online reservations are preferred. Tickets are also sold in the Visitor Center or over the phone. Prices do not include tax.

Austin Independent School District Playgrounds

There is a healthy supply of playgrounds for young ones in Austin. In addition to those in neighborhood parks (see ***City of Austin Parks***), the local school district's playscapes and outdoor facilities are open to the public after school and on weekends and holidays. The Facility Locations Map on the Austin Independent School District website can help identify those closest to you from the nearly one hundred preschool and elementary schools in the district.

Don't forget surrounding school districts too!

Multiple Locations

LOCATION Throughout the city

WEBSITE www.austinisd.org/schools

HOURS Playgrounds are available after school and on weekends when not in use by students.

ADMISSION Free

Austin Nature and Science Center

There is enough at this center to engage children for hours. So make a day of it, or break up the experience into several shorter outings. Restrooms, maps, and information are available in the Nature and Science Center's main building. Picnic tables for snacks or lunch can be found near the Trailhouse.

Austin Nature and Science Center

This building houses the Information Desk, the Naturalist Workshop, and Public Exhibits. Budding naturalists will enjoy the Workshop where the motto is "Come in—Please touch!" Magnifying glasses and a microscope are on hand for children to explore the plethora of bones, rocks, insects, shells, snake skins, and animal pelts that fill the tables and shelves. If your explorers have something interesting from nature, they can bring it to the Trade Counter and exchange their knowledge of it for points towards another item to take home with them. (See Trade Counter hours below).

The public exhibits are just around the corner. Always interactive and science-related, the themes of these rotating exhibits range from the celestial to the terrestrial. The cave exhibit is a constant though. Kids can wander through to peek at bugs in the cave walls or try to identify the animals poised above. Behind the giant glass windows in this space, kids also get an up-close view of the pond just outside.

Animal Exhibits

Exit the building to the back to find a stream-lined path that leads to the Animal Exhibits. Children can visit the resident animals that have included a bobcat, skunk, and raccoon, among other rescue animals. The Small Wonders building next door is home to smaller species. (Look up as you enter the building to find your first one!) Snakes, salamanders, toads, tarantulas, lizards, and birds make their homes here as well. Cross Nature's Way Drive to the Bird Sanctuary where hawks, buzzards, quail, and owls of all types roost.

Zilker Park Nature Preserve and Hiking Trails

Hikers can access the Preserve Hiking Trails through the Bird Sanctuary, or at two separate trailheads along Nature's Way Drive. See ***Zilker Nature Preserve and Hiking Trails*** for more details.

Dino Pit

This sand pile, the largest one in the city, hides dinosaur bones and skeletons waiting to be unearthed by young archaeologists. Shovels and brushes are provided, and educational signs about dinosaurs and the field of archaeology teach children more about their discoveries.

Classes and Camps

Check with the Information Desk for brochures on the latest happenings. Upcoming events and *Summer Camp* guides can also be found online. The Austin Nature and Science Center offers a variety of fun and educational classes for all ages, as well as family-friendly events year-round.

Zp
Zilker Park

LOCATION	2389 Stratford Dr.
PARKING	Take Stratford Dr. in Zilker Park to a dirt parking lot under the Mopac Expy./Loop 1 bridge. Cross the street and head up the hill to the Nature and Science Center.
WEBSITE	www.austintexas.gov/department/austin-nature-and-science-center
PHONE	(512) 974-3888
HOURS	Monday–Saturday 9AM–5PM Sunday noon–5PM **Trade Counter hours:** Wednesday–Friday 10AM–1PM Saturday 10AM–4PM
ADMISSION	Free

Austin Public Libraries

The public libraries house several great children's sections in twenty branches around the city. It is a great resource for board books, storybooks, reference and activity books, young adult titles, audio books, children's music, and DVDs. They also offer a variety of youth events that grow with children, from storytimes for babies, toddlers, and preschoolers, to LEGO labs and Crafternoons for school-aged kids. Spanish storytimes and pajama times can also be found on the calendar along with puppet shows, family movie nights, and young adult book clubs.

Celebrating its grand opening in 2017, the **Central Library** overlooks Lady Bird Lake and features outdoor reading porches as well as a children's crafting room, teen library, bike garage, café, and rooftop garden. It has become quite a destination spot for its amazing views, natural lighting, and award-winning sustainable architecture. The children's section is a world unto itself, a perfect space for kids to explore and socialize while being surrounded by books. Look for the giant chess game right outside its doors.

Some neighborhood favorites to check out:

Howson branch
Pair an outing to this Tarrytown library with a trip to a nearby secret—Reed Park. Hike, swim, play, and then come home to relax to a stack of books.

Carver branch
This branch shares the grounds with a playground and the ***Carver Museum*** that houses a fun, interactive exhibit on African American inventors.

Hampton branch at Oak Hill
While this branch offers engaging storytimes, the trail and pond behind the building make it a good one for active minds *and* bodies!

Twin Oaks branch

Walk through a kid-sized door into this youth library with a room of its own where child-size shelves are topped by windows. This award-winning branch for its sustainable architecture also offers a grassy hill and amphitheater out back, where kids don't have to use their quiet voices.

Multiple Locations

LOCATION, PHONE, AND HOURS

North

Milwood Branch
12500 Amherst Dr.
(512) 974-9880

Spicewood Springs Branch
8637 Spicewood Springs Rd.
(512) 974-3800

North Central

Little Walnut Creek Branch
835 W. Rundberg Ln.
(512) 974-9860

North Village Branch
2505 Steck Ave.
(512) 974-9960

St. John Branch
7500 Blessing Ave.
(512) 974-7570

University Hills Branch
4721 Loyola Ln.
(512) 974-9940

Windsor Park Branch
5833 Westminster Dr.
(512) 974-9840

Yarborough Branch
2200 Hancock Dr.
(512) 974-8820

Downtown

Central Library
710 W. Cesar Chavez St.
(512) 974-7400

West

Howson Branch
2500 Exposition Blvd.
(512) 974-8800

Old Quarry Branch
7051 Village Center Dr.
(512) 974-8860

East

Carver Branch
1161 Angelina St.
(512) 974-1010

Cepeda Branch
651 N. Pleasant Valley Rd.
(512) 974-7372

Ruiz Branch
1600 Grove Blvd.
(512) 974-7500

Terrazas Branch
1105 E. Cesar Chavez St.
(512) 974-3625

Willie Mae Kirk Branch
3101 Oak Springs Dr.
(512) 974-9920

South

Hampton Branch at Oak Hill
5125 Convict Hill Rd.
(512) 974-9900

Menchaca Road Branch
5500 Menchaca Rd.
(512) 974-8700

Pleasant Hill Branch
211 E. William Cannon Dr.
(512) 974-3940

Southeast Branch
5803 Nuckols Crossing Rd.
(512) 974-8840

Twin Oaks Branch
1800 S. 5th St.
(512) 974-9980

WEBSITE www.library.austintexas.gov
www.library.austintexas.gov/events

PHONE (512) 974-7400

HOURS Hours vary. Some libraries are closed on Sundays. The following link allows users to find branch locations, a listing of libraries open today, and an interactive map: library.austintexas.gov/locations.

ADMISSION Free

Check out these nearby libraries too:
- *Bee Cave Public Library*
- *Laura Bush Community Library*
- *Westbank Community Library*

Austin Rowing Club

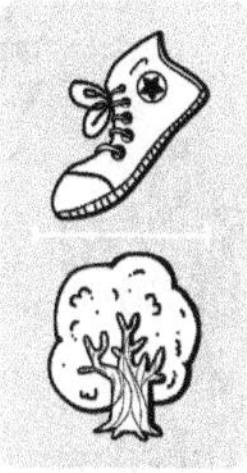

Look east from the Congress Avenue Bridge and you will spot this kayak and paddleboard rental on the lower level of the Waller Creek Boathouse. With its downtown location, Austin Rowing Club offers more urban scenery than boat rentals closer to Zilker Park. So while you will likely see less wildlife from this end of the lake, you will get a good view of skyscrapers, bridges, and Mexican free-tail bats. It's an easy paddle ride over to the Congress Avenue Bridge to listen for these winged creatures during the day. To watch them emerge, register for a guided kayak tour. Seasonal bat-watching, bird-watching, and downtown guided tours are on the calendar throughout the year too.

Tip: Allow ample time to find parking, especially if you've booked a tour.

Check in downstairs, and bring a driver license for each adult rental. Cubbies can be found both behind the desk and at the dock for storing items that you want to keep dry. The Boathouse includes a coffee shop upstairs too, so grab a drink or snack to enjoy at tables on the deck overlooking Lady Bird Lake.

Downtown Austin

LOCATION	Waller Creek Boathouse, 74 Trinity St.
PARKING	Look for curbside metered parking downtown or try the Convention Center Parking Garage at 201 E. 2nd St.
WEBSITE	www.austinrowing.org
PHONE	(512) 472-0726
HOURS	Vary by season
RATE	Kayak rentals range from $15–$25/hour or $40–$50/day, depending on size. Stand-up paddleboards rent for $25/hour.

Places to Go

Austin Steam Train

The Austin Steam Train Association re-opened passenger rail service between Cedar Park and Burnet in 1992 with its Hill Country Flyer. This scenic route to the small town of Burnet continues today with a two-hour layover for lunch on the town square and a Wild West gunfight. Passengers ride in restored cars from the early to mid-1900s. Adding to the authenticity of the experience, volunteers dressed in period clothing with a genuine enthusiasm for the rails serve as conductors, service crew, engineers, and brakemen.

In addition, shorter excursions to the historic 1912 Bertram depot and special event rides have been added to the regular schedule. Crowds of preschoolers flock to "Day Out with Thomas" when Thomas the Tank Engine visits Burnet for thirty-minute rides through the countryside followed by all day *Thomas and Friends*-themed activities and entertainment. The North Pole Flyer is another popular children's event with cookies, hot cocoa, Christmas carols, and a visit from Santa and Mrs. Claus. Other themed rides throughout the year include dinner or lunch on the train.

Ticket reservations are recommended and can be made for open-air cars, climate-controlled or first-class coaches, or lounge cars with private compartments and party rooms. Bring snacks and drinks, or visit the concession car for refreshments.

North Austin

LOCATION 401 E. Whitestone Blvd., Ste. C-100, Cedar Park

WEBSITE www.austinsteamtrain.org

PHONE (512) 402-3830

HOURS See online schedule or call the ticket office.

ADMISSION Tickets cost $23 and up depending on the event, car class, and age. Children under 3 are free if sitting in an adult's lap. Reservations are recommended; unreserved tickets are sold at the depot ninety minutes before the train departs.

Austin Zoo

The Austin Zoo and Animal Sanctuary is not your typical zoo. It is home to rescue animals ranging from pot-bellied pigs and free-ranging peacocks and roosters to lions, tigers, and bears. Visitors wander along looping dirt trails to find fox, deer, and longhorn in their natural habitats alongside a range of exotic animals that also make their home here. Children can feed deer, goats, sheep, and llamas in the Petting Zoo. For an additional fee, hop on the zoo train. The 15-minute ride on a miniature train takes you through Texas Hill Country terrain and chugs past longhorn, ostriches, and deer on the return trip. Pack a lunch to eat at one of the many picnic tables on the grounds.

West of Town

LOCATION 10808 Rawhide Trl.
The Zoo is located off of Hwy. 290 W. approximately 25 miles from downtown Austin and 2½ miles from the "Y" at Oak Hill. To get there, take I-35 or Mopac Expy./Loop 1 to Hwy. 290 W. Turn right at the stoplight at Circle Dr. Follow it for 1½ miles. Turn right on Rawhide Trl. and follow the signs to the zoo.

WEBSITE www.austinzoo.org

PHONE (512) 288-1490

HOURS **Regular hours** (February 1 – October 31):
Monday – Friday 9:30AM – 5PM
Saturday – Sunday 9:30AM – 6PM

Winter hours (November 1 – January 31):
Monday – Friday 9:30AM – 4PM
Saturday 9:30AM – 5PM

ADMISSION $13.95 children ages 2-12
$16.95 adults

Barton Creek Farmers' Market

This market is popular among Austinites for its festive scene and wide range of goodies. Located in the parking lot of Barton Creek Mall, it also boasts a nice skyline view of downtown. Live music adds to the atmosphere every Saturday as crowds browse the diverse selection of handmade crafts, locally grown fruits and veggies, organic meats, seafood, artisan breads, jellies, and yummy desserts. Kids dance and sample goodies. Check the website for upcoming events plus a detailed list of vendors and available goods.

Need more veggies? Check out the nearby Sunset Valley Farmers' Market too.

West Austin

LOCATION 2901 S. Capital of Texas Hwy.
The market is held in the parking lot of Barton Creek Mall, located at the intersection of S. Mopac Expy./Loop 1 and Capital of Texas Hwy./Loop 360.

WEBSITE www.bartoncreekfarmersmarket.org

PHONE (512) 280-1976

HOURS Saturday, 9AM–1PM

Barton Creek Greenbelt

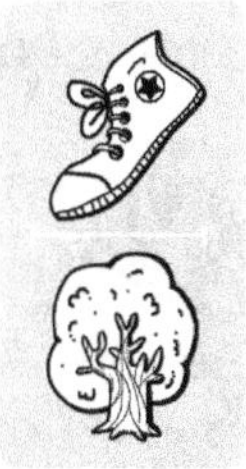

This scenic 8-mile trail runs smack dab through the heart of Austin, though you'd never know it from the lush surroundings that follow Barton Creek upstream and make one feel far from city life. The trail begins in ***Zilker Park*** (just west of Barton Springs Pool) and ends in a secluded neighborhood to the northwest off of Highway 360. There are several access points to the trail, and most hike it in parts. The best sections for young hikers are detailed below (listed in order from trail's beginning to end).

Zilker Access, *2100 Barton Springs Road in Zilker Park*
This trailhead in Zilker Park marks the beginning of the Barton Creek Greenbelt and can be found at the end of the parking lot near Barton Springs Pool. The first part of this dirt and stone trail stretches through flat, open meadowland and gradually gets greener, shadier, and closer to the water after the first ¼ mile. It's a beautiful section of the trail with several access points to the creek.

Parking: Zilker parking lot near Barton Springs Pool and the Hillside Theater.

Barton Hills Access, *2010 Homedale Drive*
This wooded neighborhood trail leads to The Flats (on the opposite side of the creek from the Zilker access point). Here, Barton Creek flows at the base of tall cliffs and over large limestone slabs. Stay to the right at the split in the trail and it's a ten-minute hike to the creek. One short section down limestone steps might be a tad steep for toddlers and slippery after a rain, but for the most part, the trail is wide, flat, shady, and very scenic. Walking beneath tall trees, you'll cross a small wooden bridge where water trickles down to Barton Creek at the trail's end. Here children can play along the rocks and in the water. When the creek is low, you can cross to the other side to access the rest of the Greenbelt.

Parking: On-street parking along Homedale Drive that runs beside Barton Hills Elementary School.

Spyglass Access, *1601 Spyglass Drive*
This entry point heads straight down a steep, but short, hill of loose rocks to put hikers 1 mile in from the Zilker Park trailhead and within ¼ mile of two swimming areas. You'll pass one of the few restrooms on the trail (a compost toilet). At the bottom of the hill and to the left, it's a very short walk on level ground to The Flats, and just a bit farther to Campbell's Hole. Both are nice spots for playing in the creek, where water flows over limestone, forming small waterfalls and pools.

Parking: Curbside.

360 Access, *3755-B Capitol of Texas Highway*
Best when the creek is flowing and you want to take a dip in it, take this section of the trail down and to the right for a ½-mile trek to Three Falls. After crossing a small wooden bridge and the 3¼-mile marker (from Zilker Park), start listening for the sound of flowing water. A short hike across the creek wash leads to a gorgeous area where the water flows over rock to form a series of small waterfalls and crystal clear pools. Shady areas lie along the bank beneath limestone overhangs. Wear water shoes and swimsuits.

Parking: You'll find a clearly marked access sign at the north end of the office park's lot that backs up to the Greenbelt.

Gaines Creek/Twin Falls Access, *3918 South Mopac Expressway/Loop 1*
This leg of the trail contains two of the Greenbelt's most popular swimming holes, Twin Falls and Sculpture Falls. The trail begins along the top of a ridge and descends to Barton Creek. The hike to Twin Falls is just under a ½ mile and while the dirt and stone path might be challenging for young children, what awaits them at the bottom of the trail makes it worth it. The terrain changes to lush creek-side vegetation and water spills over limestone outcroppings to form gorgeous pools. When the

water is up, there are some great jumping-in points, as well as plenty of shallow inlets for wading in the creek. If you're up for an additional 1 ¼-mile hike, Sculpture Falls is another beautiful swimming hole down the trail that tends to be less crowded. Bring your swimsuits.

Parking: From Highway 360, take the frontage road to South Mopac Expressway/Loop 1. Parking is available on the right near the trailhead. This trail gets crowded on spring and summer weekends, so go early.

Trail's End, *1710 Camp Craft Road*
For older children with long legs and some endurance, this steep hill of loose rock and occasional concrete slab steps, fittingly named "The Hill of Life," takes hikers down nearly 300 feet in the first ⅓ mile to surprisingly gorgeous meadowland with a waterfall spilling over the dam into Barton Creek. This trail marks the end of the Greenbelt trail. From here, Sculpture Falls is a 1 ¼-mile hike downstream. The most difficult part of this trail is going back up!

Parking: Curbside in the Lost Hills neighborhood.

Multiple Locations

WEBSITE	www.austinparks.org/park/barton-creek-greenbelt
HOURS	Daily, 5AM–10PM
ADMISSION	Free

Places to Go

Barton Springs Pool

At 68 degrees, this natural, spring-fed pool along Barton Creek is *chilly*—and a mecca for Austinites of all ages who come to sunbathe on the grassy hillside, practice flips from the diving board, swim laps, or simply soak in the cool. It's a large pool with a section for floats on the lower end where water spills back into Barton Creek and a shallower section on the upper end below historic bathhouses. There is also plenty of room for lap swimming and snorkeling throughout. The shallow end is the best spot for kids where flat limestone slabs provide a sort of beach at the water's edge and the water is not quite as cold. Bring buckets, shovels, and water toys to play with.

Zp Zilker Park

LOCATION 2131 William Barton Dr.

PARKING Several parking lots are available in the park. Meter parking is charged on weekends.

WEBSITE www.austintexas.gov/department/barton-springs-pool

PHONE (512) 974-6300

HOURS The pool is open year-round.

Friday–Wednesday 5AM–10PM
Thursday closed during the day for cleaning
Saturday–Sunday 5AM–10PM

ADMISSION Pay for tickets at kiosks near pool entrances.
$2 children 11 and under
$3 juniors 12-17
$5 adults
$2 seniors
Non-resident rates are higher.

Bat Watching

Beneath the Congress Avenue Bridge live 750,000 female Mexican free-tail bats that stream from the bridge at dusk, traveling 10 to 40 miles across the Hill Country over the course of the night. From March through October, crowds of spectators gather in the half-hour before sunset to watch them emerge from their homes in the bridge's crevices. Their numbers double to one and a half million by mid-July when babies are born, making it the largest urban bat colony in North America. The most spectacular time to see them is in August when the pups leave the nursery to hunt bugs with their mothers.

Kids with bedtimes late enough to watch these animals wake up can join the crowds of spectators on the Congress Avenue Bridge, peer up at them from a grassy area along the shore, or follow them by boat. Bat Conservation International reports expected flight times at batcon.org. Be sure to allow enough time to get a good viewing spot. To learn more about bats, check out the educational kiosks below the bridge or reserve seats on a fun, informative bat watching boat tour.

By land

Bring a blanket and set up at the Bat Observation Center alongside the lake on the southeast side of the bridge, or head onto the bridge and watch from the sidewalk as bats head off in clouds to the east.

Admission: Free

By boat

The companies listed below offer bat watching tours with commentary, making it an educational and fun field trip for the family where tourists and locals will learn interesting facts about the city and its bat population. Bring snacks and a cooler with drinks and enjoy an evening ride on the lake. Tours

*Looking for an adventurous way to watch the bats? Check out **Austin Rowing Club tours.***

last about one hour and leave thirty minutes before sunset. Reservations and early arrival are recommended. The boats are docked just below the Hyatt on Barton Springs Road. Paid parking is available in the hotel lot.

Downtown Austin

Capital Cruises

PHONE (512) 480-9264

WEBSITE www.capitalcruises.com

ADMISSION Free children under 3
$8 children ages 3-12
$13 adults
$10 seniors

Lone Star Riverboat

PHONE (512) 327-1388

WEBSITE www.lonestarriverboat.com

ADMISSION Free children 2 and under
$8 children ages 3–12
$13 adults
$11 seniors

Blanton Museum of Art

For children used to more interactive museums, the "Please don't touch" rule of the Blanton is a hard one to follow as they pass sleek Grecian sculptures that look smooth to the touch, tempting blobs of paint calling to be smooshed, and large installations seemingly waiting to be rearranged. But if you can get past this urge, or have a young babe in a sling or stroller, there is plenty to take in visually and it's an excellent way to introduce kids to great art. The interior of the building itself is impressive, with its tall, bright white walls and large box-like rooms filled with fascinating treasures and interest-grabbing imagery and color. Permanent exhibits include American and Contemporary Art, European paintings, Latin American Art, and a Prints and Drawing Gallery. Check the calendar for rotating exhibits and public events. One exhibit that is bound to enchant children is Cildo Meireles' *How to Build Cathedrals* in the Modern Art Gallery. A square pool filled with shining pennies radiates from behind transparent black curtains like a hoard of gold, illuminating the dark room and calling children to come in and touch. And in this room, they can.

Univ of Texas Area

LOCATION 200 E. Martin Luther King Jr. Blvd. (on the University of Texas campus at the intersection of Congress Ave. and MLK Blvd.)

PARKING Metered street parking is available in the blocks across MLK Blvd. in addition to several parking garages. The Brazos Garage (at Brazos St. and MLK Blvd.) offers reduced rates for museum members. Have your ticket validated at the museum. The Bob Bullock Museum's parking garage (across the street at 18th St. and Congress Ave.) and Trinity Garage (at Trinity St. and MLK Blvd.) are other options.

WEBSITE	www.blantonmuseum.org
PHONE	Main number (512) 471-7324
	Front desk (512) 471-5482
HOURS	Wednesday – Saturday 10AM – 5PM
	Sunday 1PM – 5PM
	Monday – Tuesday closed
ADMISSION	Free children ages 12 and under
	$5 youth ages 13 – 21
	$12 adults
	$10 seniors (65+)
	Tuesdays are free to the public

Bob Bullock Texas State History Museum

As visitors pass the thirty-five-foot bronze star at the museum entrance, they get a clear sense that "everything *is* bigger in Texas." The Bob Bullock houses three floors of exhibit space, an IMAX theater, the Texas Spirit theater, a café, and a gift shop. For students of Texas history, the museum is a must-see. Yet all ages will enjoy the experience, from history-loving parents and grandparents to young patrons interested in shipwrecks, revolutionary heroes, cowboys, and astronauts.

A Hall of Special Exhibitions on the first floor houses rotating exhibits. Permanent exhibits progress chronologically from the ground level up, beginning with the life of Native Americans to early explorers. Filling much of the downstairs exhibit space, you will find the hull of the French ship *La Belle*, excavated and preserved along with artifacts from the wreck. Take the stairs up to the Texas Revolution and Statehood exhibits on the next floor. The third story showcases Texas farming, ranching, and oil as well as the state's roles in World War II and the space program where children can get an up-close view of a trainer aircraft and astronaut. Another highlight: the Austin City Limits Theater features a timeline and video clips of famous past performances.

The museum theaters are also worth a visit. The IMAX shows both educational and current feature-length films. The Texas Spirit Theater runs shorter shows. One on the state's history is especially fun for its engaging special effects from lightning and fog to rattlesnakes under your seat!

Monthly family programs are offered on the first Sunday of each month when admission to the museum is free. See the online schedule for monthly themes and additional special events.

Univ of Texas Area

LOCATION	1800 N. Congress Ave. (at the intersection of Martin Luther King, Jr. Blvd.)
PARKING	Museum parking garage (at the corner of 18th St. and Congress Ave.) or curbside metered parking along the streets.
WEBSITE	www.TheStoryofTexas.com
PHONE	Main number (512) 936-8746 Tickets (512) 936-4649
HOURS	Tuesday – Sunday 10AM – 5PM Monday closed
ADMISSION	**Exhibits:** Free children ages 3 and under $9 children ages 4-17 $13 adults $11 seniors and military *Free First Sundays from 10AM – 5PM* Theater tickets can be purchased separately.

Boggy Creek Farm

Boggy Creek Farm sits on five acres with one of Austin's oldest homes used as the farmhouse, hearkening back to a time when farmers fed their neighbors and rooted communities. This sense of community is felt on market days as chefs from Austin's finest restaurants shop alongside neighbors and scores of toddlers. Children are naturally drawn to this farm with its coop full of chickens, old dump trucks and shovels for the borrowing, and room to roam. Here, they learn early on how food moves from field to market to tummies. The market stand is always filled with fresh-picked veggies, eggs, coffee, goat milk ice cream, and other natural goodies. Despite its close proximity to downtown, a trip to Boggy Creek feels more like being invited over to someone's farmhouse and asked to stay awhile.

East Austin

LOCATION 3414 Lyons Rd.

WEBSITE www.boggycreekfarm.com

PHONE (512) 920-2310

HOURS Wednesday – Saturday 8AM – 1PM
August only: Wednesday and Saturday 8AM – 1PM

BookPeople

Taking up half of the second floor of Texas' largest independent bookstore, BookKids houses one of the biggest collections of children's books in the state. Little ones race up the stairs to walls of board books, storybooks, toys, games, and activity books. Kids can find a cozy reading spot at the built-in amphitheater, or in the secret tunnel built beneath it for crawling through or curling up with a good book. Young adult readers can head to the nearby chapter book section and plop down in comfy beanbag chairs to peruse titles. Staff recommendations, classics, and award winners are prominently featured, so it is never hard to find a good read.

BookKids strongly supports its readers of all ages, so check the Event Calendar for author visits and book signings, literacy summer camps, and book clubs. For young tots, storytimes are held several mornings a week. Titles and hours can be found in the online calendar. (Get there early for a good seat, as these are popular.)

Check out Austin Recycled Reads, Black Pearl Books, First Light Books (opening summer 2023), and Reverie Books too!

Downtown Austin

LOCATION 603 N. Lamar Blvd.
WEBSITE www.BookPeople.com
PHONE (512) 472-5050
HOURS Daily, 9AM – 9PM

Butler Park

This park became popular for the Liz Carpenter Fountain, which kids quickly recognized as a giant splash pad. Set within a large circular splash area, its programmed, lighted fountains bubble and shoot water in unexpected patterns, providing kids a fun way to cool off as parents set up watch on towels in nearby grassy areas beneath the trees. Restrooms and drinking fountains are located near the parking lot alongside the Dougherty Arts Center.

While this is one of Austin's favorite splash pads, there is plenty of room to roam at Butler Park as well. A nearby pond provides good fish- and turtle-viewing. Or kids can take the short, twisting trail that circles up Doug Sahm Hill. There they will find a Texas-sized map to traverse by foot and a scenic view of Lady Bird Lake and downtown Austin.

The most recent addition is the Alliance Children's Garden filled with native plants, but the real features of the garden are the unique play areas around every corner. Looping trails lead past slides built into the hillside, swings of all sizes, rope climbing structures, and tunnels through mounded hills. Picnic tables are scattered throughout. Take sunscreen on a sunny day, as some sections of the park are unshaded.

South Austin

Location	1000 Barton Springs Rd. (in the space between the Palmer Events Center and the Dougherty Arts Center)
Parking	From Barton Springs Rd., turn north into the Dougherty Arts parking lot at the stoplight at Dawson Rd. Another option is to park in the available parking spaces along the stretch of Riverside Dr. between S. 1st St. and Lamar Blvd.
Website	www.austinparks.org/butler-park
Fountain Hours	Daily, 9AM–9:45PM
Admission	Free

Camp Mabry

Camp Mabry, an operating military post open to the public, offers a surprising range of activities for young civilians, from tank and aircraft displays to a military museum and even fishing. Extending over eight hundred acres, there is much to explore.

Texas Military Forces Museum

The Texas Military Forces Museum on the grounds houses a large display of exhibits in the former dining hall that will awe visitors, especially young ones. The exhibits span Texas' military history from early settlement to modern day. Kids can enter chuck wagons, greet soldiers on horseback, or check out the army tanks, radio communication shelters, helicopters, and airplanes. In adjoining rooms, impressive dioramas of battles from the Texas Revolution can be found. Visitors can view historical artifacts and modern military gear too.

Military Vehicle and Aircraft Displays

Just outside the museum visitors can walk down Armour Row to see an impressive array of army tanks and missile launchers. Cross the street where kids can get an up-close view of the airplanes, helicopters, and artillery displays that circle the jogging track. Visitors are also welcome in the All Faith Chapel on the corner.

Pond and Nature Trail

Bring your own bait for catch-and-release fishing in Camp Mabry's pond. To obtain an annual permit ($15 for adults), stop by the Garrison Command Building just south of the Museum and Armour Row during the weekdays. The pond sits at the bottom of the hill behind these buildings. It's a bit swampy, but there are small inlets and a bench or two along the bank for fishing (watch for snakes in the late spring and summer). If you take a right onto the dirt road near the pond, you can head upstream to the dam. Scenic and shady, you'll find a small spot along the bank here where you might drop a line. Picnic tables, restrooms, and a short Nature Trail are located in this area.

Living History Weekend

Each April, Camp Mabry hosts a living history event in honor of our military with special exhibits and reenactments. (See ***Camp Mabry Living History Weekend*** under Annual Festivals and Events.)

West Austin

LOCATION 3038 W. 35th St.
The public entrance to Camp Mabry is on 35th St., just west of Mopac Expy./Loop 1. Drive 6/10th of a mile past the old main gate (now barricaded). Go through the light at Exposition Blvd. At the bottom of the hill, just before a flashing traffic signal, turn right onto Maintenance Dr. to the gated entrance. Be sure to bring a photo ID with you, as all visitors must pass through the checkpoint at the gate.

PARKING For easiest access to the exhibits, park at the Texas Military Forces Museum.

WEBSITE www.texasmilitaryforcesmuseum.org

PHONE (512) 782-5659

HOURS **Museum**
Tuesday – Sunday 10AM – 4PM
Grounds
Open to the public during daylight hours

ADMISSION Free, museum donations are accepted

Capital MetroRail

Ticket machines, train horns, railroad crossings, engineers, giant windows, and the gentle wobble and whir of the train cars are sure to delight young passengers as they weave through parts of town never seen by car. Locals accustomed to Austin traffic will also be amazed by how quickly they can be transported south to the heart of downtown, or north from neighborhood backyards, through fields and ranch land, into the Texas Hill Country. With only nine stops along the rail's entire stretch from Leander to the Austin Convention Center, one of the nice things about this outing is how easy it is to catch a train. The online schedule is simple to read, tickets are available from a ticket machine at each station, and the rail sticks to its schedule. Keep in mind that trains run most frequently during morning and afternoon commute times. For those who are headed to a particular destination and not simply out for a joy ride, rail connector buses can be taken from most stations. Check the website for parking, schedule, and fares. No food or drink is allowed except in spill-proof containers.

Multiple Locations

WEBSITE www.capmetro.org/MetroRail

PHONE (512) 474-1200

FARES Children ride free.

Adult fares range from $3.50 for a single ride to $7.00 for a day pass.

Places to Go

Cathedral of Junk

Above the rooftops in the backyard of a small residential neighborhood in South Austin rises the Cathedral of Junk, a whimsical construction artfully arranged over the past two decades by owner Vince Hannemann. It is a place to be experienced and slowly absorbed as you wander the many levels and rooms. For adults, it can be mind boggling, both on the large scale and small. Tiny details piece together this intricately balanced structure that climbs three stories to reach the treetops with its roof framed by crutches, bicycles, and hula hoops. Kids get it right away as they jump in to climb painted bags of concrete to the top, slide down a slick tile ramp, peer through tire windows, and duck around corners to find fancy junk thrones or secret alcoves with walls of Barbie dolls, painted television sets, license plates, surf boards, Christmas lights, radios, metal coils, dangling CDs, beads, and bike chains. It's a bit precarious in places, so follow little ones closely as they explore. Older kids will love roaming the place, reentering spaces framed by new angles to offer discoveries on each pass through.

Call ahead to arrange a time to tour. Due to the Cathedral of Junk's residential location, the number of daily visitors is limited and there are some parking restrictions. Parking along nearby St. Elmo Street is preferred; if you park on Lareina Drive, be careful not to block neighbors' mailboxes and drives.

South Austin

LOCATION	4422 Lareina Dr.
PHONE	(512) 299-7413
HOURS	Monday – Saturday, by appointment
ADMISSION	Donations appreciated

Chaparral Ice Skating

Chaparral Ice is the place to go for ice skating, ice hockey, figure skating, or other ice-related sports for all ages. Introductory classes are offered, in addition to leagues, summer camps, and birthday party packages. During public skate hours, observers can watch the gracefulness of experienced skaters surrounded by the wide smiles of novices thrilled by the experience, despite their shakiness on the ice. Vending machines are available if your crew works up an appetite. Be sure to dress warm—it's chilly in there!

If you're north of town, check out the ice skating rinks at the Crossover sports complex.

North Central

LOCATION	2525 W. Anderson Ln. at Northcross Mall
WEBSITE	www.chaparralice.com
PHONE	(512) 252-8500
HOURS	Call or check the online calendar for the public skating schedule
ADMISSION	$12 adults and children $6 skate rental

City of Austin Parks

The City of Austin maintains over 250 parks, ranging from small outdoor spaces to thousand-acre tracts of parkland. From the Austin Parks Foundation website, you can search by park name for photographs and a quick overview of each park's facilities. For an alphabetical listing of all parks and trails, try the Austin Parks and Recreation website. A playground map is also available, as well as an interactive mapping feature that shows park locations and allows users to search for specific facilitiy—from covered picnic pavilions and swings to playscapes and skate parks. City of Austin Pools and Splash Pads can be found in several parks as well.

While each neighborhood recreational area has its own draw, here are some of the local favorites, each featuring several amenities:

North

- Beverly S. Sheffield Northwest District Park
- Walnut Creek Metropolitan Park

South

- Little Stacy Park that stretches along Blunn Creek to Big Stacy Park
- Dick Nichols District Park

Central

- Pease District Park
- Eastwoods Park

East

- Davis White Northeast District Park
- Bartholomew District park
- Roy G. Guerrero Colorado River Metropolitan Park

West

➤ Reed Neighborhood Park

➤ West Enfield Neighborhood Park

For the crown jewel of the Austin park system, see the ***Zilker Park*** section of this guidebook.

Check out these fun nearby parks too:
- *Play for All Park in Round Rock*
- *City Park in Rollingwood*
- *BMX skate park in Pflugerville's Northeast Metro Park*

Multiple Locations

LOCATION Throughout the city

WEBSITE www.austinparks.org

PHONE (512) 477-1566

HOURS Daily, 5AM–10PM unless otherwise noted

ADMISSION Free, with the exception of entrance fees at ***Emma Long Metropolitan Park*** and ***Walter E. Long Metropolitan Park***

City of Austin Pools and Splash Pads

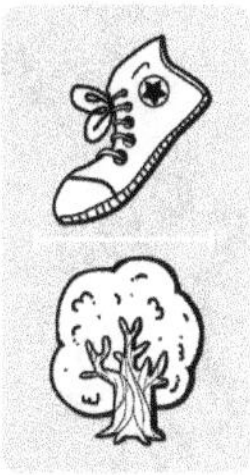

The city of Austin maintains nearly fifty wading pools, splash pads, municipal pools, and neighborhood pools, so you don't have to look far to cool off on sizzling summer days. Swim lessons and swim teams are offered at several locations. Many facilities have dedicated lap swimming hours or lanes too. The city website lists pools and splash pads by location and type and includes pool schedules. Explore hidden gems like Little Stacy's wading pool canopied by a beautiful live oak tree or the Eastwood's splash pad in a forested park where a statue of a familiar character marks the beginnings of ***Eeyore's Birthday Party***. Two other favorite splash pads among locals are located in the newly-renovated Pease Park and ***Butler Park***. For descriptions of Austin's coolest spring-fed pools, see entries for ***Barton Springs Pool*** and ***Deep Eddy Pool***.

Multiple Locations

LOCATION Throughout the city

WEBSITE www.austintexas.gov/page/pools-splash-pads

PHONE (512) 974-9330

HOURS Vary; see website for pool schedule

ADMISSION Neighborhood pools and splash pads are free.

Admission for municipal pools:

Free	children under 1
$2	children ages 1-11
$3	juniors ages 12-17
$5	adults
$2	seniors (62+)

Punch cards and passes are also available. Non-resident admission rates are higher.

Commons Ford Ranch Metropolitan Park

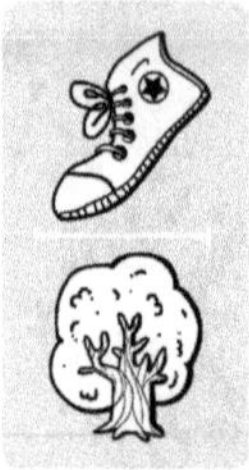

Tucked away on Lake Austin, this park is perfect for relaxing by the lake or exploring easy trails. The highlight of the park is a scenic lakeside picnic area with shoreside tables, a large open field, sand volleyball court, boathouse, and dock. Kids can play in the shallow area, watch boats pass by, fish, or explore. Also popular among pets, watch for off-leash dogs in this part of the park. A primitive restroom can be found at the top of the hill above the picnic area.

Hiking

The trailheads are not well marked, but the trails themselves are easily accessible. With the exception of the waterfall hike, the paths are jogging stroller friendly as well.

Lake Trails

The quickest way to the lake is down one of two short trails. After passing a small 1800s homestead, pull into the first shoulder to the right and park. There, you will find a scenic, wooded path behind a metal gate. Stay left to cross the footbridge and follow the creek to the lake. A smoother, more direct route can be found at the Picnic Area sign at the second shoulder to the right.

Pecan Flats Loop

Access this 1-mile loop from the lakeside picnic area. Or continue driving into the park and begin just below the ranch house. Look for an old barn, picnic gazebo, volleyball court, and open area near the trail entrance. The hike loops through restored prairie land and pecan groves with straight, wide paths and occasional educational exhibits on birds and prairies.

Have a bird-loving kid? Check out Travis Audubon's calendar that includes family-friendly birding events around town. www.travisaudubon.org

Waterfall Trail

After a good rain, you can hike upwards through cedar brush to find waterfalls. This trailhead begins near a shoulder on the left side of the main road and heads up a steeper, rockier path that extends a little over a mile to scenic views and flat rocky outcrops.

West Austin

LOCATION	614 Commons Ford Rd.
WEBSITE	www.austinparks.org/commons-ford
PHONE	(512) 974-6700
HOURS	Daily, 9AM – 10PM
ADMISSION	Free

The Contemporary Austin at Laguna Gloria

The lush twelve-acre grounds of Laguna Gloria are home to the historic Driscoll Villa and sculpture garden and serve as the outdoor complement to the Contemporary Austin's Jones Center downtown. Stone-lined paths present a scenic place for wandering along the shores of Lake Austin, with beautiful structures and art pieces cropping up in unexpected places. The outdoor venue has a distinctly European feel to it, from the 1916 Mediterranean-style villa that sits amidst carefully designed gardens to the Italian fountains and statues. Sharing the grounds with Laguna Gloria is The Art School, where you'll also find some fun art pieces and might happen upon a visiting peacock from the neighboring Mayfield Preserve.

Each month, Laguna Gloria hosts its "Second Saturdays" event to engage families in creating and experiencing art together (recommended for ages 2–11). Projects relate to the current exhibitions and have included kite making, instrument crafting, yoga, puppet shows, and live musical performances. The Art School also offers art classes year round as well as summer day camps.

West Austin

LOCATION 3809 W. 35th St.

PARKING Curbside parking available along 35th St.

WEBSITE www.thecontemporaryaustin.org

PHONE (512) 458-8191

Hours	Wed, Fri, Sat, Sun	9AM – 3PM
	Thursday	9AM – 9PM
	Monday – Tuesday	closed

Admission	Free	children under 18 and military
	$10	adults
	$5	seniors and students

Advanced reservations are available online. *Free admission on Thursdays*

Crowe's Nest Farm

Crowe's Nest is an educational working farm in Manor, a half-hour drive from Austin. Throughout the year bus loads of school groups come for field trips, and individual families are also welcome to visit. Group tours begin in the big red barn and then branch out on the surrounding paths that lead to cleverly planted children's gardens, milk cow demonstrations in the Dairy Barn, several varieties of chickens in the Hen House, and all kinds of animals, from the types one would expect on a farm—pigs, sheep, goats—to less typical residents like porcupines, emus, and llamas. For the fairy-lovers in your group, a trip to Faeriewood is in order. Walk down paths in this enchanted forest filled with fairies. Visitors can also take a tractor-pulled hayride to learn about the ostriches and bison in the fields. And a large picnic area offers a shady spot to have lunch.

Daily Tours

The farm is open fall and spring for school tours. Call ahead for reservations.

Special Events

Each October the farm opens its doors to the general public for its annual Fall Family Fun Fest. Festivities include live music, horse rides, hayrides, and food, as well as special farm demonstrations.

East of Town

LOCATION	10300 Taylor Ln., Manor
WEBSITE	www.crowesnestfarm.org
PHONE	(512) 272-4418
HOURS	Tuesday – Saturday 10AM – 2PM
ADMISSION	Free children under 2 $5 children age 2 $8 youth ages 3-12 $9 teens and adults $8 seniors 60+

Deep Eddy Pool

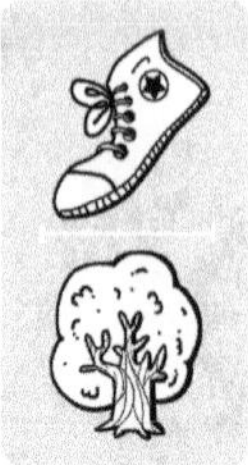

The oldest public pool in the state of Texas, its spring-fed waters rival ***Barton Springs*** in temperature, ranging from 65-75 degrees. It's the place to take young ones on a hot summer day and is a favorite among lap swimmers and families for its clear, non-chlorinated water. A zero-depth wading pool roped off at the 1-foot mark makes it ideal for the youngest swimmers. On the other side of the rope, this shallow end of the pool gradually gets up to 3½ feet, where a concrete wall divides the other end into lap swimming and a deeper recreational swim area. There is plenty of space in the surrounding lawn to set up a towel in the sun or beneath the shade of cottonwood trees.

Deep Eddy has a designated snack area near the newly renovated, open-air bathhouse. Picnic tables and a toddler playscape are also located next door at Eilers Park where you can walk down to a dock for a view of Lady Bird Lake. The trail below the pool connects to the ***Ann and Roy Butler Hike and Bike Trail*** too (at the Mopac Expressway bridge).

West Austin

LOCATION 401 Deep Eddy Ave.

WEBSITE www.austintexas.gov/department/deep-eddy-pool

PHONE (512) 472-8546

HOURS **Summer hours:**

Lap Swim 8AM–10PM
Recreational swim 10AM–9PM

This pool is open most of the year, with the exception of the first Tuesday of each month for cleaning. Check the schedule for fall, winter, and spring hours.

ADMISSION
Free children under 1
$2 children ages 11 and under
$3 juniors ages 12–17
$5 adults
$2 seniors (62+)

Non-resident rates are higher.

Dinosaur Park

Walk this nature trail and watch out for dinosaurs! The unique park features impressive, life-size, painted dinosaur figures strategically placed along a wooded gravel pathway to give children a feel for what the world must have been like when dinosaurs roamed. All ages will enjoy the scavenger hunt to search for cleverly hidden remnants from prehistoric times interspersed with the main exhibits. Young children can follow the clue numbers painted on dinosaur footprints while older children can then read the clues and help in the hunt. Educational plaques offer additional scientific facts about each exhibit. The trail is self-guided and takes about half an hour. The loop begins at the edge of a playground and picnic area and circles back to it, where children can enjoy lunch, play on the playscape, or dig for fossils in long sand tables filled with shovels and brushes. For those hooked on dinosaurs by the end, the gift shop sells a variety of dino-themed puzzles, toys, and activities.

East of Town

LOCATION 893 Union Chapel Rd., Cedar Creek
Look for the dinosaur billboard above the entrance road.

WEBSITE www.thedinopark.com

PHONE (512) 321-6262

HOURS **Regular hours:**
Wednesday – Sunday 10AM – 4PM

Summer hours:
Daily, 10AM – 4PM
Field trips and group tours are available throughout the week. Call for reservations.

ADMISSION
Free children under 24 months
$10 children 2 and up
$11 teens and adults

Dougherty Arts Center

The Dougherty Arts Center is home to a gallery and art school with classes for all ages. Young budding artists and their parents can create art together, or slightly older kids can experiment with new mediums through Saturday classes, teen programs, and after school clubs. The Dougherty also runs a popular summer camp.

The Dougherty Theater puts on several great productions for young audiences throughout the year as well. Seating 150, the space is small enough that children can feel a part of the action, and many of the performances are based on children's classics that are sure to entertain.

Look for a new, expanded arts center along Butler Shores in the near future.

South Austin

LOCATION 1110 Barton Springs Rd.

WEBSITE http://www.austintexas.gov/dac

PHONE (512) 974-4000

HOURS & ADMISSION Check website for upcoming programs and events.

Places to Go

Ella Wooten Pool

This beautiful neighborhood pool for the ***Mueller*** development opens its gates to non-residents in the afternoons. A great one for young swimmers, the shallow end is a good-sized half circle that ranges in depth from 3 inches to just under 2 feet. Mosaic fish and turtles on the pool's bottom encourage children to get their faces wet for a closer glimpse. An umbrella-shaded wall divides this end from the big pool, which starts at 3 ½-feet and gradually gets deeper towards the lap lanes at the far end.

A grassy lawn surrounds the swimming pool, and stone bathhouses can be found at the entrance. Just outside the pool gates lie a playscape, basketball court, and picnic tables.

Note: *When lifeguards are not present, resident swimming only.*

North Central

LOCATION	2047 McCloskey St. (between Pinkney St. and Mendez St.)
WEBSITE	www.muelleraustinonline.com
NON-RESIDENT HOURS	Check website for open swim hours.
ADMISSION	$2 children ages 11 and under $3 juniors ages 12-17 $5 adults $2 seniors

Other nearby pools at:
- *Patterson Park*
- *Bartholomew Park*
- *John Gaines Pool in Mueller*

Emma Long Metropolitan Park

This park makes you feel as if you've gotten away, while not traveling far at all. Emma Long rests on a long slip of land that borders scenic Lake Austin. A large swimming area with a sandy beach makes for a great, relaxing place to spend the day. Kids can swim, build sandcastles, look for seashells along the shore, jump from the docks, or bob in the waves from passing boaters. So be sure to pack the buckets, shovels, and rafts. A grove of giant oak trees and plenty of waterfront picnic tables and grills sit adjacent to this day use area, and restrooms with showers are just up the hill. The park also has sand volleyball courts, fishing, and boat ramps.

Camping is available through the online reservation system. Camping spots in the Bluff area are a bit exposed and close together with the lake in the near distance, while the spots in the Grove and Utility Area lie on the shadier end of the park, half of them waterfront. It's some of the nearest camping to be found within city limits.

If opting for lakeside drinks or dining instead of the ice chest and grill, check out nearby Ski Shores Café.

West Austin

LOCATION 1600 City Park Rd.

WEBSITE www.austintexas.gov/department/emma-long-metropolitan-park

PHONE (512) 974-1831

HOURS Day use hours are from 7AM–10PM
Park gates are locked from 10PM–7AM

ADMISSION
$5 entrance fee per vehicle Monday–Thursday
$10 entrance fee per vehicle Friday–Sunday and holidays
$10 primitive campsite (communal water only)
$20 non-shoreline utility campsite
$25 shoreline utility campsite

Note: Credit card and coin (for automated machines) only. On weekends from March–October, advance online reservations are required.

George Washington Carver Museum and Cultural Center

This museum celebrates African American culture and historical achievement through its four galleries: an interactive Juneteenth exhibit, another featuring prominent Central Texas families where visitors can examine their own family trees, a Community Gallery with rotating art exhibits, and the "Let's Pretend, Dr. Carver" Children's Gallery. Here, children can put on a lab coat and examine the many scientific advancements made by the African American community, from the first Black woman astronaut in space to the inventions of peanut butter and super soakers. A wall is dedicated to George Washington Carver that highlights his contributions to the field of agriculture. Behind the museum, visitors can follow a timeline on the sidewalk that traces Black history from the beginning of slavery in the U.S. in 1518 to the Emancipation Proclamation. In addition to these interactive exhibits, special activities and programs are scheduled for the museum's annual Juneteenth celebration. You can also combine your outing to the Carver Museum with a trip to the Carver Public Library next door or the Kealing School Park playground behind it.

East Austin

LOCATION	1165 Angelina St.	
WEBSITE	www.austintexas.gov/department/george-washington-carver-museum-and-cultural-center	
PHONE	(512) 974-4926	
HOURS	Monday – Wednesday	10AM – 6PM
	Thursday	10AM – 9PM
	Friday	10AM – 6PM
	Saturday	10AM – 4PM
	Sunday	closed
ADMISSION	Free	

Hamilton Pool Preserve

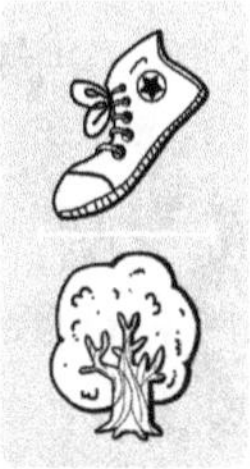

Just 30 miles west of downtown Austin, Hamilton Pool Preserve draws crowds for its cool water and scenic setting. A two-lane highway of gorgeous meadows and ranchland along Hamilton Pool Road takes you to the preserve, especially popular in the summer months for its swimming hole.

After parking just past the entrance station, you can get to the pool by taking a ¼-mile gravel and stone trail that leads from the cactus, oak, and Ashe juniper of the uplands to a creek-lined path of bald cypress, moss, and fern. Cross a small wooden bridge and a few stepping stones to arrive at the base of the grotto where a 50-foot waterfall spills from a large limestone outcropping into the pool. The flow of water depends on recent rains, but the pool level remains relatively constant (and nice and cool). Swimmers can set up towels, chairs, and picnics in the partially shady beach area where the water is shallow.

There are two restroom areas located within the park—compost toilets near the parking lot and portable toilets on the trail just before you arrive at the pool.

While most head to the grotto, you can also take a ¾-mile hike from the parking lot to the Pedernales River. Begin on the trail to the pool. Then at the River Trail marker at the base of the hill, go left to follow the creek down to the water.

A few tips before heading to Hamilton Pool with children:

➤ **Make reservations.**

Reservations are now required year round to enter the park. While taking a little foresight in planning, it guarantees entrance without the long waits of the past. Reservations can be made online for visits from 9AM–1PM or 2PM–6PM.

➤ **Call ahead.**

If you plan on swimming, call for the daily update to make sure the pool is open before driving out. A heavy rain can lead to a spike in bacterial counts or water debris and temporary pool closures.

➤ **Pack snacks and drinks.**

Food, drinks (no glass), and ice chests are allowed in the Preserve.

➤ **Leave pets at home.**

No pets are allowed in the nature preserve.

West of Town

LOCATION	24300 Hamilton Pool Rd., Dripping Springs
WEBSITE	https://parks.traviscountytx.gov/parks/hamilton-pool-preserve
PHONE	(512) 264-2740
HOURS	Daily, with reservations from 9AM–1PM or 2PM–6PM
ADMISSION	$12 advance online reservation fee per vehicle, plus $8 teens and adults $3 seniors (cash only)

Hideout Theatre

This intimate theater hidden above the Hideout Coffeeshop on Congress Avenue makes an engaging space for children to watch, and participate in, theater. The improvisational group that performs Sunday kid shows invites its audience to help join in the storytelling and acting. With an area front-and-center of the stage specifically for younger folks, it makes for easy recruiting—and quite unexpected storylines! It's great, fun entertainment for children and their parents. Acting classes and summer camps are also offered through the Hideout. (The coffeeshop makes a convenient spot to grab a snack and drinks before or after the show too.)

Downtown Austin

LOCATION	617 Congress Ave.
PARKING	Curbside metered parking is available downtown, as well as several parking lots and garages.
WEBSITE	www.hideouttheatre.com
PHONE	(512) 443-3688
HOURS	Sunday shows typically at 4PM
ADMISSION	Tickets $5

Irving and Hazeline Smith Trail

Located just up the road from the more extensive Bull Creek Trail, this hike is perfect for little legs. The 1½-mile loop trail takes hikers along an easy, well-marked, and mostly shaded dirt path. Markers along the way point out the stone wall where a Victory Garden once grew, waterfalls, and conservation lessons. The highlight is a side loop mid-way through that leads to the creek and waterfalls. Because Bull Creek is home to the Jollyville Plateau salamander, the land is protected for water quality, so no swimming, picnics, or dogs are allowed. But the clear water makes turtle spotting easy and a bench provides a good, peaceful resting spot after playing near the creek before trekking back.

West Austin

LOCATION 5343½ Old Spicewood Springs Rd.

PARKING Park in the dirt parking lot. Be on the lookout for it near the intersection of Spicewood Springs Road and Old Spicewood Springs Road. Be careful crossing to the trailhead directly across the street.

WEBSITE www.naturerocksaustin.org/greenspace/irving-hazeline-smith-trail

ADMISSION Free

Krause Springs

Krause Springs is a beautiful swimming hole and campground in Spicewood, about a half hour's drive west of Austin. The water on the property comes from cool natural springs so the water feels *fine*, especially on hot summer days.

Upon nearing the springs, ranchland and dirt road quickly give way to Hill Country oasis where streams run beneath lush vegetation under the shade of cypress trees. You can take a dip in the small but refreshing spring-fed swimming pool. A bathhouse and restrooms are located on either side of the pool with several handcrafted rock and stone picnic tables scattered beneath the cypress. Just beyond this area is a lookout point where water spills down moss-covered limestone cliffs to the swimming hole and creek below. A rather steep set of stairs and a more gradual trail both lead to the springs where limestone rocks provide spots for setting up a towel. Be careful here—the rocks can be slippery.

Bring a cooler and a raft or tube with you too. As swimmers kick back in colorful tubes and kids splash into the water from the rope swing near the picturesque grotto and waterfall, it paints an idyllic scene of summertime in the Hill Country.

If you'd like to stay overnight, primitive tent camping and RV sites are nestled a little farther down the creek under the trees. (No glass or pets are allowed.)

West of Town

LOCATION	404 Krause Spring Rd., Spicewood
DIRECTIONS	From Hwy. 71 W., turn right at the traffic signal in Spicewood onto Spur 191. Take it for half a mile. Then take another right onto County Rd. 404. The gated entrance to Krause Springs will be on your left.
WEBSITE	www.krausesprings.net
PHONE	(830) 693-4181
HOURS	Daily, 9AM – sundown Closed for winter from November 1 to February 15
ADMISSION	Free children under 4 $6 children 4–11 $10 children 12 and older and adults
DAILY CAMPING RATES	$10 children 4-11 $15 adults and children 12 and over $15 additional fee for water and electric site

Lady Bird Johnson Wildflower Center

Beautiful native landscaping, acres of gardens and trails, and Spanish style architecture make the Wildflower Center a gorgeous place to visit any time of the year. As children make their way up the entrance walk, they will undoubtedly spot the turtles and fish in the wetland pond and the deep, crystal clear pool just ahead in the center of the Courtyard. From here, children can go left to the Little House (through a child-sized door leading into a small schoolroom where nature-related books, puzzles, and art activities are always available) or head to the right to the Visitor's Gallery and Observation Tower. A nice view of the grasslands below rewards those who climb the circling stairs and ramps of the sandstone tower.

The pathways around the grounds lead through woodland gardens, theme gardens, butterfly gardens, an insectary, and the McDermott Learning Center. For those looking for additional hiking, four trails span outwards from the Wildflower Center. The shortest is the Woodland Trail, a shaded ¼-mile hike with a trailhead just below the Tower (between the library and administration building). It will take you around the Luci and Ian Family Garden to the butterfly garden and carriage house. The longest is the Restoration Research Trail, a 1-mile hike through grasslands. Maps are available online and at the admissions kiosk where you check in. Ask here to check out a Discovery Pack filled with binoculars, scavenger hunt, and activities to use while exploring the Center.

Be sure to check out the Luci and Ian Family Garden, especially with young children. The newest addition to the Wildflower Center, this garden encourages imaginative, nature-related play. Kids can climb into giant bird nests, dig in the sand pit, create with natural materials, and crawl through mosaic-lined caves and tunnels. The Watering Hole features a waterfall that spills down into small pools and a stream for playing in. This area attracts children like a swimming hole in the Texas heat. Restrooms are adjacent to the garden, and the area is stroller-friendly.

Shaded picnic areas rest in scenic spots throughout the Center. An inviting café also offers a place to cool off and enjoy snacks, drinks, or lunch while enjoying the view.

The Lady Bird Johnson Wildflower Center hosts several free, family-friendly events throughout the year. See the Events section for educational ***Nature Nights*** in the summers, Fortlandia in the fall, and ***Luminations*** during the holidays.

South Austin

LOCATION 4801 La Crosse Ave.

WEBSITE www.wildflower.org

PHONE (512) 232-0100

HOURS Daily, 9AM – 5PM

ADMISSION
Free children ages 4 and under
$8 youth ages 5-17
$15 adults
$10 seniors (65+)

Long Center

The Long Center is one of Austin's newest performing arts centers, housing a large performance hall, a studio theater, indoor community spaces, and an outdoor terrace and lawn for events, with a beautiful view of downtown from across Lady Bird Lake. The versatility of the Long Center allows for a variety of programming from the likes of Austin Shakespeare, Ballet Austin, Pollyanna Theatre Company, Austin Lyric Opera, and local musicians. Family-friendly performances and special events are scheduled throughout the year. Especially popular is the ALL summer LONG series that offers affordable (and often free) entertainment during the summer months. These fun events have included Sound & Cinema movies on the lawn as well as dances, first-rate music acts, movies on the lawn, trailer food picnics, concerts by the Austin Symphony, and ice skating on the terrace during the winter months.

South Austin

LOCATION 701 W. Riverside Dr.

PARKING The nearest parking is in the Palmer Events Center Garage at 900 Barton Springs Rd. directly behind the Long Center. Overflow parking can be found at the One Texas Center Parking Garage at 505 Barton Springs Rd.

WEBSITE www.thelongcenter.org

PHONE Box office (512) 474-5664

HOURS & ADMISSION Call or check the website for listings of events and ticket information.

Places to Go

Lou Neff Point

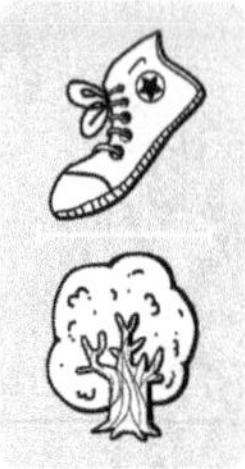

Young children flock to this spot along the Hike and Bike Trail at Lady Bird Lake to watch ducks, swans, geese, turtles, and fish. The pavilion at Lou Neff Point also provides a great vantage point for watching canoes and kayaks row by, with downtown as a backdrop. Listen for the whistle of the ***Zilker Eagle*** miniature train that chugs by regularly on the hilltop above the trail.

Zp Zilker Park

LOCATION 2000 Lou Neff Rd.

PARKING From Barton Springs Rd., turn onto Lou Neff Rd. and park in the first lot on the right. Head down to the Hike and Bike Trail along the lake and go left. It's a short walk to the pavilion.

ADMISSION Free, with the exception of metered parking on weekends

Mayfield Park and Preserve

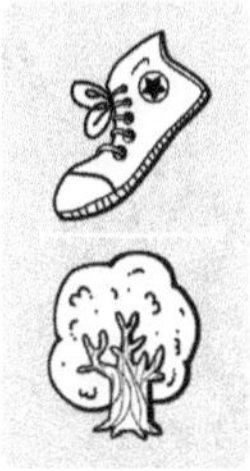

Mayfield is a wonderful place to wander with children. Peacocks roam freely, welcoming visitors to the historic cottage and gardens. Winding rock pathways lead past lily pad-filled ponds, beautiful gardens, old stone structures, and towering palm trees in the expansive courtyard. It offers young visitors a world of discovery.

Beyond the stone wall enclosing the cottage grounds lie picnic tables and over twenty additional acres to explore. The trailhead nearest the cottage takes hikers through easy, wooded trails to Lake Austin, across Taylor Creek, and to the base of limestone cliffs. Another trailhead lies at the west end of the parking lot near the chimney swift tower and portable restrooms. Taken right, it leads towards Laguna Gloria, or go left to connect with the other trails. The hikes are all fairly short. Due to the wildlife in the park and preserve, no pets are allowed.

West Austin

LOCATION 3505 W. 35th St.

WEBSITE www.austintexas.gov/department/mayfield-park

PHONE (512) 477-1566

HOURS Daily, dawn to dusk

ADMISSION Free

McKinney Falls State Park

This state park is a popular one with creek access, a hike and bike trail, and overnight camping less than half an hour's drive from Austin. With nearly 750 acres to play in, it's perfect for daytrips or weekend camping. Check in at the entrance station to find out about park events, from ranger-led fishing to guided hikes. Park maps are also available at the Headquarters and in the Smith Visitors Center where kids can touch animal pelts, create nature crafts, and check out exhibits about the area.

Onion Creek flows through the park, providing wading, fishing, and swimming. At both the Upper and Lower Falls, water spills across limestone slabs to form swimming holes. Be sure to inquire at the office about the suitability of swimming as bacterial counts can occasionally spike after heavy rains.

A shady stretch with a number of fairly secluded tables along the wooded Onion Creek Hike and Bike Trail make a perfect spot for picnics. The paved 2.8-mile trail provides great biking for all ages too (with just a couple of steep hills). Older children might enjoy the new 1-mile mountain bike trail or the isolated Homestead Trail, accessible by crossing the Lower Falls.

For hiking, stop in the Smith Visitors Center to pick up a guide map to the nearby Rock Shelter Interpretive Trail, an easy ¾-mile loop trail. Start on the creek side for a lush, shaded hike under large cypress trees, across wooden bridges, and beneath a beautiful, large rock shelter that extends over the trail. Little legs may want to turn back here, or continue on (stay to the right) to travel back through more exposed meadowland.

Overnight camping is also available. You can choose from eighty-four water and electric sites clustered beneath trees; eight hike-in, water-only sites along the creek; six shelters; or a youth group area. Call ahead for reservations (for all except hike-in campsites).

East of Town

LOCATION	5808 McKinney Falls Pkwy.
DIRECTIONS	From Austin, take Hwy 183 S. to McKinney Falls Pkwy.
WEBSITE	www.tpwd.state.tx.us/state-parks/mckinney-falls
PHONE	(512) 243-1643
RESERVATIONS	(512) 389-8900 www.tpwd.state.tx.us/business/park_reservations
HOURS	Daily, 8AM–10PM
ADMISSION	Free children 12 and under $6 teens and adults for day use
CAMPING FEES	$20 campsites with water and electricity (30 amp) $24 campsites with water and electricity (50 amp)

McKinney Roughs Nature Park

McKinney Roughs is a beautiful LCRA Park located between Austin and Bastrop. A short jaunt from the city, it offers 18 miles of hiking trails ranging from rugged Texas Hill Country and bluffs to piney canyons and shady, wooded trails along the Colorado River. It's a great hiking destination with well-maintained trails and grounds.

Check in at the Visitors Center to pick up a park map that lists all trails and their mileages along with suggested hikes and approximate times for completing them. Children will enjoy observing the Center's impressive fish, turtle, snake, and salamander habitats or examining bits of nature at the touching table. Just outside the building, scenic paths loop among educational exhibits. For those with a bit more endurance, hit the hiking trails with water, snacks, sunscreen, and hats packed.

Be sure to check the park calendar for fun community and educational programs too. Stargazing, moonlight rafting, ziplining and ropes courses, scavenger hunts, and camps are offered throughout the year.

East of Town

LOCATION	1884 Hwy. 71 W., Cedar Creek
WEBSITE	www.lcra.org/mckinneyroughs
PHONE	(512) 303-5073
HOURS	Daily, 8AM – 5PM
ADMISSION	Free children 12 and under $5 teens and adults $2 seniors (65+)

Mexic-Arte Museum

Mexic-Arte has been bringing Mexican, Latin American, and Latino art to Austin for nearly forty years. While the three exhibit spaces are primarily adult-focused, a good time to check out the museum with children is on Family Days. Admission is free on Sundays too, and special tours are offered. The museum also hosts ***Viva La Vida Fest*** each fall, a popular annual event to celebrate El Día de los Muertos, or the Day of the Dead. (See entry in the Annual Events section).

Check out the Mexican American Cultural Center's community events, gallery, after school clubs, and summer camps too. www.austintexas.gov/esbmacc

Downtown Austin

LOCATION 419 Congress Ave.

WEBSITE www.mexic-artemuseum.org

PHONE (512) 480-9373

HOURS

Monday – Thursday	10AM – 6PM
Friday – Saturday	10AM – 5PM
Sunday	noon – 5PM

ADMISSION
$1 children 12 and under
$7 adults
$4 seniors and students
Free on Sundays

Millennium Youth Entertainment Complex

Upon entering the Millennium, parents of the 80s and 90s will feel as if they've taken a step back in time when weekends were spent skating to Michael Jackson, eating snack bar pizza, and hitting the arcades. Built in 1999, the youth entertainment complex houses a bowling alley, roller skating rink, food court, and video arcade. The alley offers sixteen lanes of bowling with side bumpers available for young bowlers and a food court nearby. Skaters of all ages take over the rink, complete with laser lights, music, and plenty of room to roll. The arcade is decent-sized with games ranging from toddler-age merry-go-rounds and auto racing videogames to air hockey and billiards. Owned by the City of Austin and run by a private company, costs are kept at a minimum. Birthday party and group packages are also available.

East Austin

LOCATION 1156 Hargrave St.

WEBSITE www.myec.net

PHONE (512) 472-6932

HOURS Wednesday – Saturday 10AM – 10PM
Sunday – Tuesday closed

Mount Bonnell

The highlight of this short hike is the impressive view of Lake Austin and the hills from atop Mount Bonnell. For kids excited about stairs, they can climb the long rock stairway to the top, or little legs can take a more gradual route up the gravel path from the far north end of the parking lot. Giant limestone slabs line this end of the trail where hikers can glimpse the Pennybacker Bridge in the distance or watch ski boats speed by below. (Keep an eye on toddlers since the area off of the trail here is rather steep.) A few picnic tables are scattered around the park and short side trails lead to secret, hidden spots among the trees as well as to a scenic view of the Austin skyline at the far south end. No restrooms are on site, but it's a short trek up and back.

West Austin

LOCATION 3800 Mount Bonnell Rd.

WEBSITE www.austinparks.org/covert-park-at-mt-bonnell

PHONE (512) 477-1566

HOURS Daily, 5AM–10PM

ADMISSION Free

Mueller Farmers' Market

That the Mueller Farmers' Market has become one of the city's largest and most vibrant comes as no surprise. With families within walking distance and locals coming for the playgrounds, trailer eatery, and hike and bike trail, it posed an organic complement to the neighborhood. The market is housed in the Branch Park Pavilion and spills out onto sidewalks, green space, and adjoining streets.

Definitely the best farmers' market in town for kids, Mueller provides a playground with unique play structures, an extensive splash pad area, and open space to run and dance. With live music playing, it's a great place for a picnic. Good eats can be found aplenty in the market stalls—from ethnic, vegan, and gluten-free foods to delicious desserts. Also for the picking are wines, flowers, preserves, farm-fresh veggies, grass-fed beef, and coffees and teas. If you want to stick around even after vendors close shop, there is plenty to do nearby. (See ***Mueller Parks and Trails***, ***Ella Wooten Pool***, ***The Mueller Skate Park***, or the ***Thinkery***.)

North Central

LOCATION 2006 Philomena St.

PARKING Curbside metered parking is available as well as two nearby parking garages: Texas Mutual Garage across the street (with entrances on Philomena and Aldridge Streets) and the McBee Garage (with entrances on McBee and Robert Browning Streets).

WEBSITE www.texasfarmersmarket.org/mueller

HOURS Sunday, 10AM – 2PM

Mueller Parks and Trails

At Mueller Lake Park, just across the street from the ***Thinkery***, children float through the air on giant, saucer-shaped swings. They climb on rubber, rope, and metal; spin on geometric contraptions; and balance on a rotating beam that serves as a merry-go-round. It's a fun playscape, unique from most in Austin. For young ones, there is a smaller playscape that overlooks the lake. Restrooms are located just outside the gate to the enclosed playground area. Picnic tables can be found by the playscapes and scattered along the nearby lake trail, where catch-and-release fishing is a popular activity.

The neighborhood offers a range of activities for families. Just beyond the playground, the paved trail provides a perfect place for children to bike, trike, scooter, or wander around the lake to feed the ducks and geese. Those with more endurance can continue along the decomposed granite trail that winds for 5 miles throughout the Mueller development—past large, metal spider art pieces, waterfalls spilling into ponds, and native grasslands.

Several additional playgrounds and picnic spots are also located nearby. Near the Mueller Retail Center, a beautiful trellised picnic area provides shade within close sight of a playscape. In the southwest section of the neighborhood lies parkland with a basketball court, playground, picnic areas, and ***Ella Wooten Pool***. In the southeast Greenway, you'll find the ***Mueller Skate Park***. Look for more spaces to play as this neighborhood continues growing.

North Central

LOCATION 4550 Mueller Blvd. The Mueller Neighborhood is located on the site of Austin's former Robert Mueller Municipal Airport, along the east side of Airport Blvd.

WEBSITE www.muelleraustin.com/park-events

Mueller Skate Park

Located in the expansive Southeast Greenway, the Gaylor Sackler Memorial Skate Park lies across from green space on a fairly quiet stretch of the Mueller development, with the exception of the sounds of whizzing wheels, shifting gears, and the grating of small scooters on gravel sidewalks. As you get closer, you can hear the smooth whoosh of skateboards as they bob and coast along cement and the clack of wheels landing tricks.

The park accommodates all ages—toddler to adult. Young riders pedal and scoot along sidewalks that wind past picnic areas and through parkland. Novice BMX riders and skateboarders test their skills on the short beginner loop while those with more experience can hit the longer intermediate track. For tricks, a separate area features a half bowl with railings, ramps, and skate stairs. A staging area with benches sits just in front of the restrooms.

North Central

LOCATION 3601 Zach Scott St.
WEBSITE www.muelleraustin.com
HOURS Daily, 5AM–10PM

The Natural Gardener

The Natural Gardener provides more than pots, plants, and garden tools. Along the edges of its eight acres grow beautiful demonstration gardens. So while this nursery is not necessarily for kids, per se, it can make a good outing for kids with parents who like to dig in the dirt. Children will enjoy meandering down paths past fountains, through creatively-planted garden beds, and over small wooden bridges. At the trail's end, kids will be especially delighted to find two resident goats and a coop full of chickens. A labyrinth and even more gardens lie directly behind the corral of pots, directly across from the gift shop.

Specializing in native plants and organic gardening, this garden shop offers classes, online resources, and helpful information printed on each pot. With its location on the outskirts of town, a visit can seem like an escape from the city — to be surrounded by plants. That said, it's best to go early in the morning on the weekends or on a weekday if you want to avoid parking congestion and crowds of weekend gardeners.

West of Town

LOCATION 8648 Old Bee Caves Rd.

WEBSITE www.tngaustin.com

PHONE (512) 288-6113

HOURS Tuesday – Sunday 9AM – 5PM
Monday closed

9th Street BMX

Located in the heart of the city on the south side of Duncan Neighborhood Park, this BMX trail was community-built over the years by local riders. This same communal spirit is felt in the welcoming vibe of the park that attracts all ages and levels. Riders are encouraged to abide by the unspoken laws of the land, namely: be observant and go with the flow, be friendly, respect others on the trail, and take care of the place. Designed for a range of skill levels, beginners roll and bob along a series of small dirt mounds while advanced riders catch air and perform tricks on higher, built-up ramps. Older kids might want to check out the nearby BMX Skate Park on 12th Street too.

Downtown Austin

Location	900 W. 9th St.
Website	www.9thstreetbmx.com
Hours	Daily, 7AM–10PM
Admission	Free

Northern Walnut Creek Trail

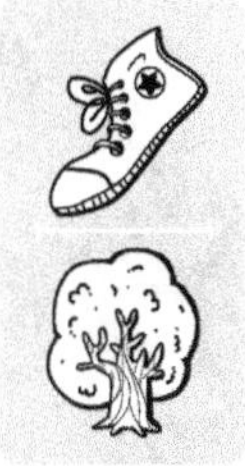

This paved, tree-lined path begins at Walnut Creek Metropolitan Park to stretch 3.2 miles to Balcones District Park, with another access point midway at Gracywoods Neighborhood Park. With the exception of two steep areas, this mostly flat, two-lane trail makes for easy going by either bike or stroller. Scenic and fun, it winds along wooded Walnut Creek, crosses nine bridges, dips below a wooden railroad bridge, and passes giant concrete pillars beneath Loop 1 to connect recreational areas. Each of the parks along the trail has a playground and green space for rest stops or snack breaks as an added bonus. Northern Walnut Creek Trail is a good one for mixed ages and modes of transport. In fact, if you want to take things up a notch, try one of the many hiking and mountain biking trails throughout the metro park.

North Austin

LOCATION **Trailhead** – 12138 N. Lamar Blvd. at Walnut Creek Metropolitan Park. Park across from the baseball fields and look for the metal, railed entrance that marks the beginning of the bike path. Restrooms are located nearby.

Middle Access – 12133 Metric Blvd. at Gracywoods Neighborhood Park

Trailhead – 12017 Amherst Dr. at Balcones District Park

WEBSITE www.austintexas.gov/page/walnut-creek-trail-system

HOURS Daily, 5AM–10PM

ADMISSION Free

Pedernales Falls State Park

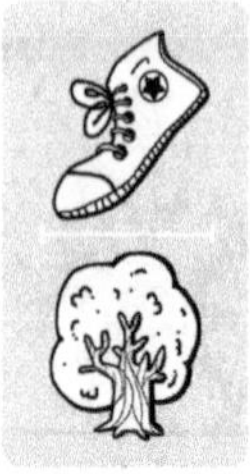

Though less than an hour's drive from the fast pace of the city, you'll feel as if you have gone much farther when all that can be seen from scenic overlooks are trees and river; deer can be spotted walking just beyond your campground; and unlike many nice hikes in Austin that carry the constant roar of traffic, all that can be heard here is the roar of water after a heavy rain.

Pedernales Falls, one of the most popular destinations in the park, lies on the north end. A short hike on gravel leads to a scenic overlook of the falls, which can be quite impressive depending on recent rains. Water levels vary with the weather, but the beach area tends to be a great place for all ages to hike along the boulders, wade in the river, collect seashells, build sandcastles, or play in spring-fed pools. Keep a lookout for herons and other wildlife drawn to the water. Farther down the river, tubing is a popular summertime activity.

The Bird Blind and Star Theater are additional areas that nature lovers will enjoy. Entering the birding shelters, you can sneak a peek from behind glass windows at an amazing numbers of birds of all kinds flitting about in their native habitats. Labeled photos teach visitors which species they are seeing. Next door, star parties are regularly held. Check at headquarters or the online event calendar for dates.

For short, scenic hikes with the kids, head to the campgrounds. The Twin Falls Nature Trail loops behind campsites #13 and #21 and leads to an overlook with a beautiful view of the falls spilling over a cliff into the creek below. Trammell's Crossing Trail near campsite #33 passes the park amphitheater and is an easy walk down to the river. If the water is low enough, hikers can cross to a long strip of beach area to play. Older children might enjoy the 4 miles of hiking and mountain biking on the other side through Hill Country terrain.

The campgrounds provide nice camping if you decide to stay awhile. A cluster of seventy fairly isolated, good-sized sites are located in the middle of the park surrounded by trees, each with a shaded picnic table and grill. Restrooms and showers are nearby.

West of Town

LOCATION	2585 Park Road 6026, Johnson City
DIRECTIONS	From Austin, take Hwy. 290 W. through Dripping Springs. Turn right onto FM 3232 and drive 6 miles to the park entrance.
WEBSITE	www.tpwd.state.tx.us/state-parks/pedernales-falls
PHONE	(830) 868-7304
RESERVATIONS	(512) 389-8900 www.tpwd.state.tx.us/business/park_reservations
HOURS	Daily, 8AM–10PM The park occasionally closes for wildlife management activities so call ahead or check the park's website before heading out.
ADMISSION	Free children ages 12 and under $6 teens and adults for day use
CAMPING FEES	$20 camping sites with water and electricity $10 primitive sites (hike-in, 2-mile min.)

Peter Pan Mini-Golf

This local business has been family owned and operated since 1948. Its charm lies in the relaxed atmosphere as golfers putt through the legs of timeless characters like Peter Pan and a giant T-Rex, through the mouth of a whale, or under unique pirates, turtles, and lighthouses. With two 18-hole courses to choose from, the area is small enough that kids can easily do both. The east course is slightly less challenging with fewer uphill holes. It is a bit more maze-like though, and golfers have to pay attention to the number for the next hole (good counting practice for younger kids, and if you get out of order, no one seems to mind). The west side is more clearly laid out with a number of iconic figures. While the course can get a bit hot on sunny afternoons, ice chests are allowed (without glass) and sno-cones are sold at the ticket counter. Or to make it an even more Austinesque day, head east just up the street to the ever-popular ***Sno-Beach*** on Barton Springs Road.

South Austin

LOCATION 1207 Barton Springs Rd.

WEBSITE www.peterpanminigolf.com

PHONE (512) 472-1033

HOURS Vary by season

ADMISSION **One course (18 holes):**
$7 children 5 and under
$9 adults and children 6 and over
Both courses (36 holes):
$12 children 5 and under
$14 adults and children 6 and over

Pinballz

There is a novelty and simplicity to this old-school arcade that makes it fun for all ages. For kids, it is a mini-Vegas where they can rush excitedly among the buzzing hum and blinking lights in search of the machine that will spew the most tickets or offer the most candy to grab. Parents will be amazed to find Atari with old joysticks, pinball scoreboards that flip, character-themed games from the 80s and 90s, and classics like Millipede, Space Invaders, Tron, and Q*bert. As its names suggests, Pinballz also features an impressive number of pinball machines. Most are for sale, which guarantees a rotating selection of surprises each time you visit.

The original Pinballz opened in 2010. Since then, the owners have created two other locations—one north and one south. The original spot feels the most classic, with coin- and token-operated machines, a prize counter, snack bar style food, and a BYOB policy. Party rooms and event spaces are available by reservation.

North Central

LOCATION 8940 Research Blvd.
PHONE (512) 420-8458
WEBSITE www.pinballzarcade.com
HOURS Monday – Friday 11AM – 10PM
Saturday – Sunday 10AM – 10PM
Open later for ages 18+

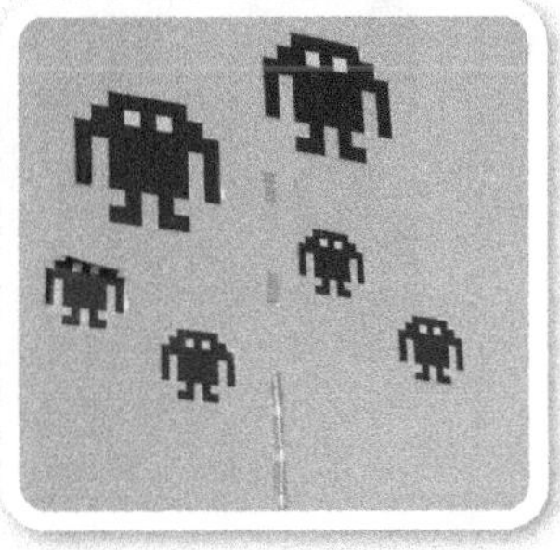

Pioneer Farms

Visitors take a trip back in time to farm life in the mid- to late-1800s as they step onto the grounds of this ninety-acre outdoor museum. Stop in the General Store to pick up a free Walking Tour brochure to guide you along the ¾-mile path that loops around the farm. Group tours are offered on weekends. Head out to experience history come alive on a German immigrant homestead, in a wooded Tonkawa Indian Camp, and at an old Settlers' Cabin. You'll pass chickens in the henhouse and cow, pig, and donkeys in the corrals. A working blacksmith shop near the Scarborough Barn holds demonstrations on weekends. Continue on to visit the Cotton Planter's homestead with a kitchen and spinning room out back. There are several good spots for a picnic lunch, and restrooms for Menfolk and Womenfolk can be found throughout the park.

Before leaving, be sure to grab a copy of the *Pioneer Farms Gazette* with news and upcoming events, or check the website for camps, special demonstrations, reenactments, and homeschool and scouting days scheduled throughout the year.

North Austin

LOCATION	10621 Pioneer Farms Dr.
WEBSITE	www.pioneerfarms.org
PHONE	(512) 837-1215
HOURS	Thursday–Sunday 10AM–5PM
ADMISSION	Pay in the General Store
	Free children ages 2 and under
	$6 youth ages 3–17 and seniors
	$8 adults

Play for All Park

Though technically in Round Rock rather than Austin, this park for all abilities merits a visit. A paradise for imaginative play, it features a large playground area adjacent to a kid-sized speedway and recreated Round Rock town center. So, load up the trikes, training wheels, and big wheels for the younger set. With pedal power, kids cruise down mini-streets lined with road signs and controlled by stoplights. Pop in the local library or refuel at the Wag-a-Bag, visit a police and fire station, make adjustments at the mechanic, or go through a car wash with real misters.

The playground itself minimizes chaos through its separated play areas. Kids gravitate to spaces according to their interests, whether to the rock band pod, sensory sand play space, or accessible playscape and swings.

Just below the park, older bikers can hop on the Brushy Creek East Trail that winds 3 miles farther east along the creek. Other kid-friendly access points on the more extensive Brushy Creek West Trail include Champion Park and Brushy Creek Lake Park.

North Austin

LOCATION 151 North A. W. Grimes Blvd., Round Rock

WEBSITE www.roundrocktexas.gov/city-departments/parks-and-recreation/play-for-all-park

PHONE (512) 452-1901

HOURS Daily, 6AM–midnight

Playland Skate Center

Playland Skate Center houses Austin's largest skating rink, complete with flashing lights, glittery disco balls, and a range of music. Handrails line the entire rink at a child's level, with plenty of openings for skaters to get on and off to rest on benches against the walls. For those who need some practice before feeling comfortable on the big rink, a small children's skate area is set apart at the rear of the building. Lessons are also available. A small arcade and snack bar keep younger, non-skating siblings occupied.

North Central

LOCATION	8822 McCann Dr.	
WEBSITE	www.playlandskatecenter.com	
PHONE	(512) 452-1901	
OPEN SKATE HOURS	Thursday	3PM – 8:30PM
	Friday	3PM – 10PM
	Saturday	noon – 8:30PM
	Sunday	noon – 5PM
	Mon – Wed	closed
ADMISSION	$12 skate rentals	
	Sk8 for $8 discounts on Thursdays	

River Place Nature Trail

Found in a hilly subdivision in west Austin, this scenic creek trail is part of the Balcones Canyonland Preserve. The two lower woodland trails — the Lower Panther Trail and the Fern Creek Trail — are both shady and easy enough for young hikers. They are also the best marked around, with maps and a kiosk at every junction.

The best hike for kids begins at the boardwalk, near an informational kiosk and small pond. The short wooden pathway takes hikers along the water's boundary to the dirt path and log steps of Lower Panther Trail, a ½-mile hike through shaded woods along Panther Hollow Creek. Wooden bridges, stepping stones, and surprises at every corner keep children engaged, whether they discover another set of log steps, idyllically placed benches, turtles in the clear creek, or waterfalls spilling down moss-covered limestone cliffs after rains.

After the first ½-mile, you might turn back where the trail forks and return the way you came, or decide to continue just a bit farther, up Fern Creek Trail, to a beautiful, clear pool at the base of a small waterfall. A nice wide bench overlooking the pool makes a good spot to look for turtles and rest. Older children may wish to continue the last ½-mile before heading back, but the going does get steeper.

For teens with stamina, another option is the challenging 5.5-mile round-trip Canyon Trail. This path takes you into the heart of the preserve through a steep climb above Panther Hollow Creek with beautiful Hill Country overlooks.

Upon returning, cross the street to Woodlands Park for restrooms with water fountains, a playground, and picnic tables along the creek.

West Austin

LOCATION	9000 Big View Dr. (across the street from the soccer fields and playground at Woodlands Park)
PARKING	Curbside or in the parking lot at Woodlands Park.
WEBSITE	www.riverplacelimiteddistrict.org/trails.html
HOURS	Daily, dawn to dusk
ADMISSION	Free children ages 12 and under $10 teens and adults on weekends Credit card only

Round Rock Express Baseball

Round Rock Express games are an easy family-friendly outing just a short drive from Austin. Minor League baseball fans will love it, but there is plenty for kids to like about going to these games in addition to the sport. For little ones with energy, there is room to roam in the Lawn Seating, or below the Porch section. Be sure to pack a blanket, sunscreen, and baseball hats for "seats" in these areas. The team mascot, Spike, also wanders through the crowds greeting young fans. And a Fun Zone for kids eight years old and younger contains a playscape, bouncy house, and sport court. Entrance to this area is free, although there is an admission fee for the rock wall and bungee trampolines. Hot dogs, cotton candy, pizza, ice cream, and other baseball fare are available throughout the park. At the end of the games on Sundays, kids are invited to run the bases. Check the schedule for the firework displays too, following the games on Fridays and other select nights.

North Austin

LOCATION	The Dell Diamond, 3400 E. Palm Valley on Hwy. 79, Round Rock
WEBSITE	www.roundrockexpress.com
PHONE	(512) 255-2255
ADMISSION	Tickets start at $10 and vary by section. Children 2 and under are free.

Rowing Dock

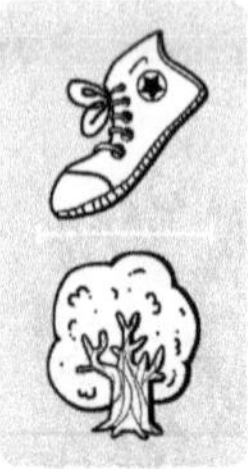

The Rowing Dock is easy to spot from the Mopac bridge with its brightly-colored kayaks and stacks of rowing boats on Lady Bird Lake. This boathouse puts paddlers in on the quieter, less-trafficked west end of the lake. Head upriver beneath scenic cliffs and keep your eyes open for herons along the banks and stacks of turtles sunning themselves on logs. Kayaks, pedal kayaks, canoes, and stand-up paddleboards are available to rent by the hour. Onsite parking makes the dock easy to get to with kids, and a picnic table and portable restroom are on site. On nice weekends, boating can be a popular activity, so it's best to go early to avoid long waits. Bring a driver's license and a credit card for deposit. Cubbies are available for storage.

Zp
Zilker Park

LOCATION 2418 Stratford Dr. (just west of the Mopac Expy./Loop 1 bridge on Stratford Dr.)

PARKING Spaces are available in the gravel parking lot directly above the rental dock.

WEBSITE www.rowingdock.com

PHONE (512) 459-0999

HOURS **Summer hours**
Daily, 9AM – 8PM (last rentals at 7PM)

Winter hours
Daily, 9AM – 6PM (last rentals at 5PM)

RATE Rentals range from $20 – $30/hour or $45 – $65/day

St. Edward's Trail

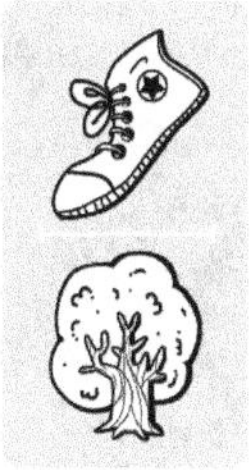

If you have young children with you, it might be best to approach this 3- to 4-mile loop trail (with several spurs and side shoots) by choosing the type of activity you would like to do rather than trying to complete it all in one trek. With its varied terrain, St. Edward's Trail can easily be viewed as three distinct hikes: through open meadowland (north of the creek), along Bull Creek, and up a wooded path atop the bluffs (south of the creek). There are two main trailheads with a parking lot at each: a smaller one with a sign noting St. Edward's Trail, and a little farther up the road, a larger lot with a kiosk, map, and trailhead.

Meadow Trail

Head right from either trailhead to hike through level, open prairie land grasses and wildflowers. It's an especially pretty hike in the spring. Take a left at any juncture to move from fields to creek.

Creek Trail

St. Edward's Trail is most fun for playing in the creek, especially after a good rain when the water is flowing. The trailhead from the smaller parking lot leads to a shady bank along the water (from the larger parking lot and trailhead, simply head left) where children can wade, race leaves and sticks in the current, or cross on large stepping stones to the bank on the opposite side. Just a bit farther up the trail, an old dam divides the water into pools and provides scenic views up the creek as well as good turtle and fish spotting. Continue on the trail to a waterfall that spills

over bluffs into a limestone pool. From here, you can keep to the trail to eventually loop through the more exposed meadow trail or head back along the creek.

Hill Trail

If you have any hikers in your group with some endurance, they might enjoy crossing the creek (take the trail downstream from the dam to a bank with stepping stones) to the south end of the park that rises above the creek through wooded Ashe juniper and oak. It's a scenic trek up the hill as you climb limestone steps and tree roots, with gorgeous views of the creek and fields below. (Young hikers need to pay attention where the trail hugs the edge in places.) While the rise in elevation might become a bit much for little legs, it can be a peaceful and rewarding experience for those who appreciate a steeper rise in elevation than that offered by most trails in the area.

West Austin

LOCATION	7301 Spicewood Springs Rd.
PARKING	There are two parking lots: a small area on the shoulder of the road with a sign for St. Edward's Trail and a larger parking lot with a map and kiosk.
PHONE	(512) 974-6700
HOURS	Daily, 5AM–10PM
ADMISSION	Free

Scottish Rite Children's Theater

Scottish Rite puts on fun children's theater. Most of the productions are adaptations of classic children's tales, made shorter and more interactive for young audiences. The Scottish Rite, formerly a German opera house built in 1871, is home to the oldest operating theater in Austin, seating 250 patrons on the lower level and as many children as will fit on the large carpets front and center of the stage where they can become active participants in the plays. The sets are always impressive and the stories silly and engaging. Afterwards, theater-goers are often invited to meet the cast on stage or in the parlor where they set up with pen and posters to sign autographs.

Downtown Austin

LOCATION 207 W. 18th St.

WEBSITE www.scottishritetheater.org

PHONE (512) 472-5436

HOURS & ADMISSION Call or check the website for the season's schedule and ticket information.

Places to Go

South Congress

The trendy strip of South Congress Avenue just south of the river draws both tourists and locals to its funky, eclectic mix of boutiques, fun shops, and good eats. Also known as SoCo, it's a great place to stroll the sidewalks and window shop. Visitors will especially enjoy strolling the aisles of Allen's Boots, and kids will want to eye all the goodies inside ***Big Top Candy Shop***. If you get hungry, grab a bite at ***Home Slice Pizza*** with ***Amy's Ice Creams*** or Jeni's Splendid Ice Creams for dessert.

Not big shoppers? Head to Jo's Coffee to take a family photo at the iconic "i love you so much" graffiti wall and grab drinks or snacks to go. Then head to nearby Little Stacy Park for some playground action or creek exploring!

South Austin

LOCATIONS Strip of S. Congress Ave. between Riverside Dr. and Oltorf St.

PARKING Curbside along Congress Ave. and neighboring streets (watch for Resident Parking Only signs), or the parking garage behind Guerro's Restaurant at Congress Ave. and Elizabeth St.

Southern Walnut Creek Trail

This paved hike and bike trail provides 7.3 miles of continuous two-lane pathways absolutely free of cars that makes it great for kids. Stretching from the Austin Tennis Center at one end to Govalle Park at the other, it winds its way through normally unseen parts of east Austin, running along scenic green space. Trees line the trail and occasional pools of water, creeks, and river create a lush landscape.

Well marked with regularly posted mileage signs (that approximate biking and walking minutes to the next stop too), the trail connects Govalle Park, Davis White District Park, and the East Communities YMCA—all with playgrounds. Or stick to the path and pedal past meadowland, city overlooks, baseball fields, and a golf course to cross bridges and follow creeks to the Colorado River. With several access points (see map), you can choose the best location and distance for your crew. Then pack the scooters, trikes, or bikes and hit the trail!

Watch for the Northern Walnut Creek Trail expansion too!

East Austin

LOCATION **North end**–7800 Johnny Morris Rd. at Austin Tennis Center

Middle access–5315 Ed Bluestein Blvd. at East Communities YMCA

South end–5200 Bolm Rd. at Govalle Park

WEBSITE www.austintexas.gov/department/southern-walnut-creek-trail

TRAIL MAP www.austintexas.gov/page/walnut-creek-trail-system

HOURS Daily, 5AM–10PM

ADMISSION Free

Splash! Exhibit

This exhibit is perfect for science-minded children of all ages. Interactive displays inside this simulated limestone cave allow them to test water quality, peer in fish and salamander tanks to see what life swims in local creeks and rivers, pretend to navigate a mini-submarine in search of water contaminants, watch a short film about Barton Springs on a cave wall, and create thunderstorms at the push of a button to learn about human impact on watersheds. Even leaving is made fun as visitors exit through a sliding wall of bubbling water.

Zp Zilker Park

LOCATION	2201 William Barton Dr. (in the Sheffield Education Center to the right of the Barton Springs Pool entrance)	
WEBSITE	www.austintexas.gov/department/beverly-s-sheffield-education-center	
PHONE	(512) 974-6350	
HOURS	Tuesday – Saturday	10AM – 5PM
	Sunday	noon – 5PM
	Monday	closed
ADMISSION	Free, with the exception of metered parking on weekends	

Terra Toys

Terra Toys is a toy store that welcomes play. Children pass by on fire trucks and plasma cars or pushing child-sized shopping carts. Gongs, tambourines, and egg shakers sound from the musical instruments section as impromptu bands form. Brio trains clack along wooden tracks on the play table. With ample space for playing and browsing, this independently-owned shop carries a wide range of areas with kid appeal: arts and crafts, scientific exploration, imaginary play, transportation, performance art, games and puzzles, and outdoor activities. Babies have a special area devoted to them, and a fairly extensive collection of storybooks is housed in the rear of the store, along with stuffed animals and puppets. If you need a pick-me-up, stop by the in-store coffee shop that serves tasty drinks and ice cream. Be prepared to spend more time here than expected.

For comic books and board games, Dragon's Lair Comics & Fantasy is just around the corner too.

North Central

LOCATION	2438 W. Anderson Ln.	
WEBSITE	www.terratoys.com	
PHONE	(512) 445-4489	
HOURS	Monday – Saturday	10AM – 7PM
	Sunday	noon – 6PM

Places to Go

Texas Memorial Museum

This museum will fascinate both children and adults. The trek up a tree-lined slope of steps from the west to this white, fossil-filled fortress, or past dinosaur tracks and a bronze saber-toothed cat from the east marks a passage from this world to one that existed millions of years ago. Upon entering the museum, visitors' attention is immediately arrested by the giant Texas Pterosaur with a forty-foot wingspan that looms overhead. More such exhibits and educational displays fill each of the four floors. Don't miss the Onion Creek Mosasaur in the Hall of Geology and Paleontology that swims among a collection of giant sloths, armadillo ancestors larger than you ever imagined, ancient amphibians, and collections of bones and fossils sure to impress youngsters. The Hall of Texas Wildlife, one floor up, houses more familiar insects and animals from barn owls and rattlesnakes to roadrunners and coyotes. A newly revamped exhibit space with interactive activities can be found on the top floor.

How many floors you get to and how long you stay at each will depend entirely on your child's interest and age. Regardless of how much you see on a particular visit, it is one of those museums that will contain something novel and interesting each time you go. Be sure to check the museum website for fun, science-oriented events for children hosted throughout the year.

Univ of Texas Area

LOCATION	2400 Trinity St. on the University of Texas campus (two blocks north of the UT stadium)
PARKING	San Jacinto Garage next door to the museum at 2401 San Jacinto Blvd.
WEBSITE	www.texasmemorialmuseum.org
PHONE	(512) 471-1604
HOURS	Tuesday – Saturday 9AM – 5PM
ADMISSION	Free UT faculty, staff, students Free children under 2 $5 children ages 2-12 $7 teens and adults

Texas State Capitol

The Capitol is a good place for exploring with kids of all ages, from blanket picnics with babies on the lawn, to roaming with toddlers, to leading young ones up the Great Walk lined with cannons and statues of Texas heroes to enter the giant doors of the Capitol. All will be struck by the enormity and grandiosity of the building, but it is also intriguing to see it from a child's perspective where life-sized marble statues and governors' portraits are eyed with wonder, and maze-like hallways of polished granite lead to hidden elevators and secret chambers. Be sure to head to the rotunda to spin under the star in the dome and test the acoustics. Take a peek in the House and Senate chambers. You might also want to visit the underground Capitol Extension where you can grab a snack or meal in the Cafeteria.

Pick up brochures for Self-Guided Tours of the Grounds or the Capitol building or get them online: www.tspb.texas.gov/plan/tours/tours.html. Free, guided tours are offered throughout the day and last about forty-five minutes. Check with the Treasurer's Business Office on the first floor for times.

Visit the Capitol Visitors Center for more history — and to see the Goddess of Liberty through a telescope.

Downtown Austin

LOCATION 1100 Congress Ave.

PARKING Two hours of free public parking are available at the Visitor Parking Garage at 1201 San Jacinto St. (barring any special events). Curbside paid parking is also available along surrounding streets.

WEBSITE www.tspb.texas.gov/prop/tc/tc/capitol.html

PHONE (512) 463-0063

HOURS Monday – Friday 7AM – 8PM
Saturday – Sunday 9AM – 8PM

ADMISSION Free

Texas Union Underground

You rarely see a bowling alley like this one—it glows. Head to the bottom floor of the Texas Union student center on the University of Texas campus and enter a bowling alley where disco balls and black lights illuminate toothy grins, neon-colored laces on bowling shoes, and neon pink, orange, and yellow bowling balls as they roll down the lanes during glow ball hours. This alley features twelve lanes with programmable bumpers for younger bowlers, in addition to billiards, foosball, and air hockey. Families and college students tend to be the most common patrons, although the two groups' schedules rarely overlap, so the lanes usually aren't crowded until after children's bedtimes. Snacks are available at the front desk (candy, ice cream bars, chips, and sodas), or head to the food court on the Union's main floor. While there's plenty of good bowling in Austin, this one adds a neat spin to the sport.

Univ of Texas Area

LOCATION Texas Union building at 24th St. and Guadalupe St. on the University of Texas campus, in the north corner of the bottom floor

PARKING San Antonio Garage (25th St. and San Antonio St.) is the nearest parking garage, one block away. The university is also well served by Capital Metro and has plenty of bike racks, so consider taking a bus, shuttle, or bikes to avoid the hassle of campus parking.

WEBSITE www.universityunions.utexas.edu/food-fun/texas-union-underground

PHONE (512) 475-6670

HOURS

Monday – Thursday	10AM – 11PM
Friday – Saturday	10AM – 10PM
Sunday	noon – 10PM

Special Glow Ball Hours:

Thursday – Friday after 5PM
All day Saturday and Sunday

The Union Underground observes the university schedule to some extent, so call ahead around holidays and semester breaks to confirm times.

RATES **Regular bowling** (per game/per person)

$3 Monday – Wednesday
$3 Thursday – Friday (before 5PM)
$4 Thursday – Friday (after 5PM)
$4 Saturday – Sunday

$2/pair bowling shoe rental

Thinkery

As this popular children's museum touts, the space is perfect for children ages zero to eleven. The layout offers plenty of room to explore, and the exhibits attract kids by age and interest. As children develop, they gravitate towards age-appropriate areas while discovering a variety of ways to interact with old favorites—whether in the kitchen science lab, the hands-on inventor's workshop for young makers and builders, the healthy living market and Move! Studio, a cozy book nook, the aquatics discovery area, an outdoor courtyard with a nature play space and multi-story jungle gym, or in any of the rotating exhibits. All stations encourage learning and cooperation.

Babies and toddlers can find a safe haven to explore too, protected from the excited bigger kids racing by, in sections of the Let's Grow and Currents exhibits reserved exclusively for them. During designated Baby Bloomer hours, babies and tots also have the run of the museum, as only three-year olds and younger are admitted. Special storytimes, sing-a-longs, and activities geared for young children are scheduled.

The Thinkery also organizes regular storytimes (some bilingual), engineering projects, spring break and summer camps, and special events throughout the year. Check the online calendar for details.

North Central

LOCATION	1830 Simond Ave.	
WEBSITE	www.thinkeryaustin.org	
PHONE	(512) 469-6200	
HOURS	Tuesday	9AM–7PM
	Wednesday–Thursday	9AM–3PM
	Friday–Sunday	10AM–5PM
	Monday closed (except for Baby Bloomers)	

Baby Bloomer Hours *(for children 3 and under)*
Monday, Saturday 8AM – 10AM

ADMISSION
Online reservations recommended
Free children 0-23 months
$18 24 months and up

Memberships available

Community Nights, entrance by donation

Tuesday 3PM – 7PM
Sunday 3PM – 5PM

Tower Garden

When on the University of Texas campus with kids, the Tower Garden is worth seeking out. This series of ponds filled with fish, turtles, and lily pads will delight young children as turtles pop up their heads to greet them or stack themselves on rocks to sun. The garden, which lies just north of the UT Tower, is dedicated to the memory of victims of the Tower Shooting of 1966, but most young visitors know it affectionately as the "Turtle Pond."

Univ of Texas Area

LOCATION Between 24th St. and the north side of the UT Tower (directly behind the Biological Laboratories building)

PARKING Two of the nearest visitor parking garages are the San Antonio Garage located three blocks west (25th St. and San Antonio St.) and the San Jacinto Garage (24th St. and San Jacinto Blvd.).

Places to Go

Toy Joy

$

What strikes one upon entering this toy shop is the sheer number of toys packed into every nook and cranny. Toy Joy is one of those rare places where all ages play together, testing out wacky costumes, goggling over 80s action heroes, or perusing the many bins of timeless party favors (made even more unique through clever and creative signage). Specializing in the fun and nostalgic, Toy Joy offers the latest in pop culture while staying true to old favorites: rubber animals, action figures, games and puzzles, puppets, costumes, pranks, and an amazing assortment of plastic animals. It's apparent that the owners and staff have fun with their inventory, and you'll find toys here that you won't find anywhere else in town.

Multiple Locations

LOCATION, PHONE, AND HOURS

Downtown

403 W. 2nd St.
(512) 320-0090

Monday – Thursday
10AM – 9PM

Friday – Saturday
10AM – 10PM

Sunday
10AM – 9PM

North Central

4631 Airport Blvd.
(512) 904-0209

Monday – Thursday
10AM – 9PM

Friday – Saturday
10AM – 10PM

Sunday
10AM – 9PM

WEBSITE www.toyjoy.com

Toybrary Austin

Ideal for six-month-olds to five-year-olds, Toybrary is a genius of an idea. This toy lending library offers families a sustainable way to keep kids engaged in educational play through a constantly refreshed supply of "new" toys, without having to purchase or store them. Members can check out items, stay and play with the many active and imaginative toys in the store, head to the backyard for outdoor play, attend special events and workshops, or sign up for drop-off childcare or a Parents' Night Out. Non-members have access to many of the same services, with the exception of toy loans. A community space in many ways, Toybrary Austin also houses a preschool, music classroom, and separate rooms for birthday parties and camps. Check the online calendar for parent workshops and an ever-changing list of events to engage young children. It is a great space to meet up with other young families, socialize, and play.

North Central

LOCATION 2001 Justin Ln.

WEBSITE www.toybraryaustin.com

PHONE (512) 765-4174

HOURS Tuesday – Saturday 10AM – 6PM
Sunday – Monday closed

Turkey Creek Trail

On this wooded trail through the Texas Hill Country, kids will enjoy the level terrain, the shade provided by the canopy of trees, and the excitement of leaping on stepping stones across Turkey Creek, which the trail crosses at several spots. For parents, this trail offers the feel of getting out of the city without having to travel far. If you have a dog, bring the family pet along too. As a no-leash zone, this is a popular hike for dog owners.

The entire trail is 2.7 miles long. After ¾ of a mile, the trail splits. It becomes a loop that moves from limestone creek bed surrounded by fern-covered canyon walls to a short climb to the top of a cliff for a brief walk through more arid, exposed terrain before heading back down into the trees to the original trail. With the exception of this one short climb, the hike is fairly level. The full length of the trail may be a bit much for little legs, but simply turn around at any point for a shorter outing. Or take a left where the trail splits to go to the Fern Wall and listen for the burble of flowing water or rest on a bench or boulder and just enjoy being out. The scenery makes any length trek worth the trip.

For restrooms, a picnic, or a swim in Lake Austin afterwards, drive 1 mile farther up City Park Road to ***Emma Long Metropolitan Park***.

West Austin

LOCATION 1600 City Park Rd.

PARKING Park in the dirt lot at the trailhead. Spots are most difficult to come by on weekend mornings when the trail is busiest.

ADMISSION Free

Umlauf Sculpture Garden

Featuring the works of Charles Umlauf, this beautiful outdoor museum combines art and nature seamlessly. Babies will like the stroller ride beneath tall, shady cottonwoods and toddlers will be thrilled to roam along the gravel paths. Children of all ages will find the waterfall, streams, and ponds appealing as they cross bridges and wander pathways leading past strategically placed sculptures, from a cluster of intriguing animals to the boy "Diver" poised to plunge into the pond where a couple embraces in "The Kiss." Ask at the front desk for the scavenger hunt that transforms the exhibit into an engaging quest.

Storytimes, family activities, tours, and art workshops for a range of ages are also offered throughout the year. Check the website or call for programs and dates.

Zp
Zilker Park

LOCATION 605 Azie Morton Rd.

WEBSITE www.umlaufsculpture.org

PHONE (512) 445-5582

HOURS

Tuesday – Friday	10AM – 4PM
Saturday – Sunday	11AM – 4PM
Monday	closed

ADMISSION

Free	children ages 12 and under
$1	youth ages 13-17
$7	adults
$5	seniors (60+)

Free Second Sundays for Family Days

University of Texas Star Party

For stargazing within the city limits, head to the rooftops of The University of Texas. Star parties are held on Wednesdays at the top of Robert Lee Moore Hall (RLM) and on Fridays and Saturdays atop Painter Hall. Best for older kids able to squint one eye when looking into a telescope and to wait patiently in line for their next glimpse of the moon, stars, nebulous gases, or planets, the entire experience can be quite a fun venture.

For a midweek star party with a technologically advanced, 16-inch telescope that features automatic tracking and dome rotation, take the elevator up to the top floor of the RLM. There, the search for the observatory becomes a scavenger hunt to follow the telescope signs pointing to additional stairwells, down hidden hallways, and through mysterious doors. At the top of the final stairwell, open the door onto a fenced rooftop where the cityscape presents its own impressive nighttime display. The event is an informal, come-and-go affair. University graduate students and professors with an obvious enthusiasm for astronomy are on hand to point out celestial objects and answer questions. While you wait between turns to peer into the telescope, enjoy the view!

The telescope mounted in the smaller domed roof of Painter Hall is equally impressive—for its simple mechanics and history. To find this weekend night star party, climb the stairs to the top floor; follow the signs up metal, ladder-like stairs; and arrive at a pair of short, blue doors straight out of Alice and Wonderland. These open to a dark, circular room topped by a dome. The telescope

sits in the middle, aimed at a narrow slit in the ceiling that opens to the night sky. The astronomer peaks out the nearby window to find celestial objects, swivels the telescope, and moves the dome into alignment by hand crank. Visitors then take turns climbing a large wheeled ladder to gaze into the 9-inch instrument. It's a more intimate space that engages kids' attention on many levels.

Before you go, check the weather. If it's cloudy or rainy, call the number listed below for possible weather cancellations.

Univ of Texas Area

LOCATION **Wednesdays:** Robert Lee Moore Hall (RLM) on the University of Texas campus

Fridays and Saturdays: Painter Hall on the University of Texas campus

Check the website for specific directions to reach each telescope.

PARKING At night, curbside parking can usually be found along Dean Keaton St. (formerly 26th St.) right across from the RLM Hall and a few blocks from Painter Hall; see the website for parking garage information.

WEBSITE http://outreach.as.utexas.edu/public/viewing.html

PHONE (512) 232-4265

HOURS When the university is in session, viewings occur from 7PM–9PM or 8:30PM–10:30PM, depending on the season. Check the website for specific dates and times.

ADMISSION Free

University of Texas Tower Tour

If you have ever been curious about the view from the UT Tower, tours take visitors up twenty-seven floors by elevator and three more by stairs to an observation deck that offers an amazing panorama of the city. Kids will like the bird's eye view of the University of Texas campus, the Capitol, downtown, and tree-filled neighborhoods and hills that stretch to the edge of town. Chest-high walls along the deck and metal railings that extend overhead make the area safe, although shorter children may need a boost to see out. Binoculars are for the borrowing and cameras and cell phones are permitted. Mid-way through the forty-five minute tour, guides offer a short talk to those interested about the architectural design and function of the building and then give groups a little more time to look around and ask questions before the tour's end.

Reservations are recommended. Visitors are advised to arrive twenty minutes early to pick up tickets from the Hospitality Center in the Texas Union. Tickets are released to those on the waitlist ten minutes prior to the tour. No purses, backpacks, or bags are allowed. Leave them behind, or you can rent a locker at the Hospitality Center for $1 to store your belongings.

Univ of Texas Area

LOCATION Tours are in the Main Building on the University of Texas campus. Pick up tickets in the Texas Union (located on Guadalupe St. between 22nd and 24th Sts.) at the Hospitality Center (on the south end of the main floor).

PARKING Parking in the University Co-op garage at 23rd St. and San Antonio St. or the San Antonio Garage at 25th St. and San Antonio St.

WEBSITE www.universityunions.utexas.edu/food-fun/tower-tours

PHONE (512) 475-6633

HOURS The schedule varies with the university's calendar. Check the online schedule or call for tour days and times.

ADMISSION $6 per person

Veloway

Biking on smooth pavement in the Hill Country sans cars makes an outing to the Veloway worth the trip, especially for young bikers. The 3-mile loop (that can be shortened to 1 mile with a shortcut) winds through wooded scenic green space in the Circle C Metropolitan Park just up the street from the ***Lady Bird Johnson Wildflower Center***. Open exclusively to cyclists and skaters, the trail runs one-way in a clockwise direction, with slower traffic staying to the right. Picnic tables and open areas along the way provide good rest stops, or keep pedaling and enjoy the fun of being on a road with only human-powered traffic. Portable toilets and a water fountain are located near the entrance.

South Austin

Location	4900 La Crosse Ave.
Website	www.austintexas.gov/department/veloway
Hours	Daily, dawn to dusk
Admission	Free

Walter E. Long Metropolitan Park at Decker Lake

Stretching along the southern end of Lake Walter E. Long, a sizeable 1,200-acre lake in east Austin (also called Decker Lake), this long slip of a park on the waterfront offers picnicking, swimming, and fishing with access points at several coves and inlets along the bank. If you come to fish, there is a bait shop just outside the park gate. Be sure to pick up a map and brochure from the entrance station that lists the most common types of fish caught as well as the state bag and length limits. A boat ramp and two docks are also located in the park, as well as several good spots for putting in a kayak or canoe.

East Austin

LOCATION	6614 Blue Bluff Rd.
WEBSITE	www.austintexas.gov/page/lake-walter-e-long
PHONE	(512) 926-5230
HOURS	Daily, 5:30AM–10PM
ADMISSION	$5 per vehicle Monday–Thursday $10 per vehicle Friday–Sunday $1 per person walk-ins

Note: Credit card and coin (for automated machines) only.

Westcave Outdoor Discovery Center

Westcave Outdoor Discovery Center offers a self-guided trail through the Uplands, guided weekend hikes to a gorgeous grotto area with a waterfall, educational field trips, and monthly star parties.

Guided Canyon Tour

One of the most beautiful trails in the area, this 1-mile hike provides enough ecological and terrain diversity to keep children's interests, from wandering along flat, flower-lined paths to a scenic overlook at the top of the Canyon Trail, down stone steps (hold onto the handrail) to the natural springs burbling into the Pedernales River. The highlight of the hike is a gorgeous, lush grotto and waterfall adjacent to the cavern that gives Westcave its name. Two distinct ecosystems overlap along this hike, making it unique in that a wide variety of vegetation covers the 1-mile trail, from cactus and wildflowers to lush ferns and brilliant mosses. The trees also range from Ashe juniper and sycamore to impressive six hundred-year-old bald cypresses classified in the giant sequoia and redwood families.

To protect the area, the trail is only accessible to the general public during weekend tours. The guide adds much to the trek, leading groups behind the waterfall and into the cave while helping spot the endangered golden-cheeked warbler who lives here in the spring. (Binoculars are available for loan from the Educational Learning Center.) The entire tour lasts approximately one hour and fifteen minutes.

With the forty-five minute drive from Austin, the venture can turn into a half-day event, and one well worth it.

Arrive early as tours are limited to the first thirty people. While you wait, have a picnic and scope out the Educational Learning Center or the Uplands Trails. (Be sure to wear appropriate shoes for the hike too; the area near the waterfall can be a bit slippery.) No pets are allowed in the preserve.

Uplands Trails

The trails in the Uplands area start from a boardwalk near the Educational Learning Center and traverse easy, scenic prairie land filled with bird habitats. The Juniper Trail Loop covers .4 miles, or continue on the 1-mile Prairie Trail Loop. Maps are available as you check in, though the trails are well marked.

Star Parties

Forty-five minutes west of downtown, Westcave Preserve gets fairly dark skies and hosts star parties several months of the year. Astronomers set up telescopes near the Environmental Learning Center shortly before dark. As the first stars of the night appear, they point out constellations and direct their telescopes to the moon, planets, star nebulas, and the Milky Way to give visitors a closer glimpse of the universe. Registration is required and limited to thirty guests so that everyone has an opportunity to use the telescopes. Book early! Bring chairs, snacks, drinks, and a flashlight.

Next door, Reimers Ranch also holds star parties from their observatory. Reservations required: https://parks.traviscountytx.gov/reimers-observatory

West of Town

Places to Go

LOCATION 24814 Hamilton Pool Rd., Round Mountain

DIRECTIONS From Austin, take Hwy. 71 west to Bee Cave. Turn left onto Ranch Rd. 3238/Hamilton Pool Rd. at the traffic light. After 14 miles, you'll cross the Pedernales River. The entrance to the Preserve is the next gate to the right.

WEBSITE www.westcave.org

PHONE (830) 825-3442

Uplands Trails and Educational Learning Center

HOURS Reservations are available online

ADMISSION $5 per person

Guided Weekend Canyon Tours

HOURS 9AM, 11AM, 1PM, 3PM
Check online calendar for availability

ADMISSION *includes access to Upland Trails*
Free children under 4
$10 children 4-15
$20 adults

Star Party

HOURS Dark, time varies by season.

ADMISSION Free children under 4
$10 children 4-15
$25 adults
Registration required:
www.westcave.org/specialty-hikes

Whole Earth Provision

For a camping and adventure specialty store, Whole Earth offers a surprisingly amazing selection of quality toys—especially ones that teach about the outdoors or that get kids out in it. In fact, their toy section has been slowly expanding over the years, claiming more and more retail space. While this is the place to go for nature and science-related toys like kites, magnets, astronomy kits, bug collecting boxes, binoculars, butterfly nets, and volcanoes, you can also find puppets, baby-friendly items, art supplies, bath toys, and activity books. Whole Earth has a unique, well-culled book section too with fun, slightly offbeat picture books and plenty of science-related titles for all ages. It's a perfect store to buy gifts, stock up on travel kits for road trips, or go play around a bit. Another plus is the friendly staff who wholeheartedly embrace the company philosophy to "Have fun!"

Multiple Locations

LOCATION **Downtown**
1014 N. Lamar Blvd.

PHONE (512) 476-1414

HOURS Monday – Saturday 10AM – 6PM
Sunday noon – 6PM

LOCATION **South**
Westgate Shopping Center
4477 S. Lamar Blvd.

PHONE (512) 899-0992

HOURS Monday – Saturday 10AM – 8PM
Sunday noon – 6PM

WEBSITE www.wholeearthprovision.com

Places to Go

Wild Basin Wilderness Preserve

The Wild Basin spans 227 acres and forms part of the larger Balcones Canyonland Preserve. Despite the sound of traffic in the distance and the few houses you pass on the hillside above the trail, overall you get the feeling that you are out in the Texas Hill Country as you traverse down rocky trails, climb limestone steps, cross Bee Creek, and pass under cover of cedar and oak trees. The ¼- to ½-mile hike (depending on whether you choose the south or north access point) that leads to the Waterfall is the highlight of this series of trails. Be prepared for more exposure on the south side, while the north entrance leads down shady, tree-covered paths.

With 2½ miles of hiking trail to choose from, and many of them looping, you can easily modify your nature walk to a length that matches your group's endurance. The ½-mile Arroyo Vista Loop is also stroller friendly.

Take a photo of the map posted at the trailhead, or pick one up in the Environmental Education Center. The center offers monthly interpretive hikes and educational programs for small groups as well. *Pets and bikes are not allowed.*

West Austin

LOCATION 805 N. Capital of Texas Hwy.

WEBSITE www.stedwards.edu/wild-basin

PHONE (512) 327-7622

HOURS Daily, sunrise to sundown

ADMISSION Free on weekdays.
Reservations required on weekends and holidays for a nominal fee.

ZACH Theatre

Recently remodeled, the Zachary Scott Theatre located along the banks of Lady Bird Lake is home to locally produced plays and musicals as well as those of international renown. Family-friendly shows are often performed in the intimate, 130-seat theater in the round, making the experience especially engaging for audiences. ZACH's emphasis on youth engagement with theater is apparent from their season schedule and educational outreach, in addition to their growing campus to accomodate classes and camps offered throughout the year.

South Austin

LOCATION 202 S. Lamar Blvd.

WEBSITE www.zachtheatre.org

PHONE (512) 476-0541

HOURS & ADMISSION Call or check the website for the season's schedule and ticket information.

Zilker Botanical Gardens

The Botanical Gardens are a wonderful place to visit with children of all ages. With winding paths through flowers, ponds, butterflies, and even dinosaurs, visitors may roam for as long as they would like, or break up the experience into several short outings. Four areas with the most kid-appeal are listed below. Trail terrain varies with each section, moving from pavement, to brick and stone, to decomposed granite, but the paths are stroller-friendly just about everywhere except the Japanese Garden. Maps and restrooms can be found at the Garden Center.

Japanese and Rose Gardens

The Japanese Garden lies just below and to the east of the Garden Center. Gentle streams flow alongside stone paths, through waterfalls, and into clear lily pad- and turtle-filled ponds. Parents will perceive the peacefulness of this garden while the secret pathways, stepping stones, wooden bridges, and bamboo overlooks on the trail make it exciting for children, full of pleasant discoveries.

Past the koi pond and gazebo, visitors enter the Rose Garden. From here, you can stay on the trail to follow metal dinosaur tracks on the

fence to the Prehistoric Garden, or head left to take the gently sloping sidewalk through terraced beds of roses and native flowers to the Pioneer Settlement and Butterfly Trail.

Pioneer Settlement and Butterfly Trail and Garden

A peek into the blacksmith shop, a furnished log cabin, and a one-room rural schoolhouse give children a glimpse into the lives of settlers from nearly two hundred years ago. On select weekends, blacksmiths fire up the furnace and offer living history demonstrations. Iron butterfly benches nearby provide a good resting spot and mark the beginning of a trail filled with flowers and springtime butterflies.

Hartman Prehistoric Garden

This garden is a favorite among children. As they follow the dinosaur tracks etched in the stones set along the circular pathways, their imaginations can run wild. Trekking through this simulated dinosaur "habitat" of palm trees, ferns, lily pads, and a waterfall, they will discover a large sculpture of a dinosaur feeding in the middle of a pond. If kids look closely, they may also discover non-extinct animals in the water too.

Zp
Zilker Park

LOCATION	2220 Barton Springs Rd.
WEBSITE	www.zilkergarden.org
PHONE	(512) 477-8672
HOURS	Vary seasonally
ADMISSION	Online reservations required. Free children 2 and under $3 children ages 3-17 $6 adults $5 seniors (62+) Non-resident admission rates are slightly higher.

Zilker Eagle

There is something ageless about riding the Zilker Eagle. Babies, toddlers, young children, parents, and grandparents enjoy the simple excitement and rhythm of it as life slows down to the pace of a miniature train. The Eagle makes a twenty-five minute loop from the station through the north end of the park. Along the route, passengers can look for turtles, fish, ducks, and swans in Lady Bird Lake while passing under the bridge on Barton Springs Road. The track continues above the hike and bike trail with scenic views of the lake, park, and downtown. Most exciting for the kids is the home stretch where the train slips beneath a bridge on the Zilker playscape and through a tunnel before returning to the train depot.

In 2021, after retiring the beloved Zilker Zephyr, the new Zilker Eagle was built and fresh tracks were laid. Unexpected delays have kept the Eagle from flying, but look for it on the tracks soon.

Zilker Park

LOCATION 2100 Barton Springs Rd., located between the playground and Barton Springs Pool

WEBSITE www.zilkertrain.org

HOURS Train runs on the hour on weekdays and every half-hour on weekends. Opens at 10AM. Last train leaves at 7PM in spring-fall and at 5PM in winter.

PHONE (512) 477-1566

ADMISSION Cash only. An ATM machine is on site.
$2 "littles" (ages 1-11)
$3 "bigs" (children over 12 and adults)
$2 "well earned" (ages 65+)

Zilker Nature Preserve and Hiking Trails

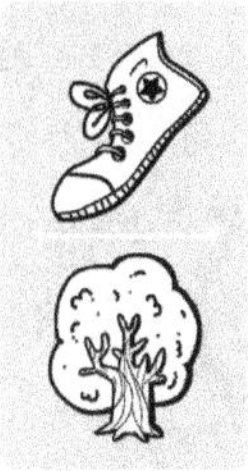

The Zilker Nature Preserve is one of those "smack dab in the middle of Austin" spots that has the power to make the city magically disappear as soon as you step into it. How far you can get along the trail with your little ones depends on their age, endurance, the temperature, and the length of their legs and attention spans. With the exception of the rock steps that lead down to the entrance of the main trailhead and a few switchbacks up to Lookout Point, the trails are mostly flat and easy. The entire area might be viewed as one large trail that takes hikers from one setting to another, from the shade of Texas mountain laurels and cottonwood trees to limestone cliffs topped with prickly pear cactus that overhangs creek beds to treks through sunny wildflower-filled meadows. But it is divided into a series of several short, marked trails with different access points. So you can always choose one for the day and take your time about it. Maps are posted at the trailheads.

Note: No pets are allowed in the preserve.

Informational markers dot the area, along with reminders to children and their guides to:

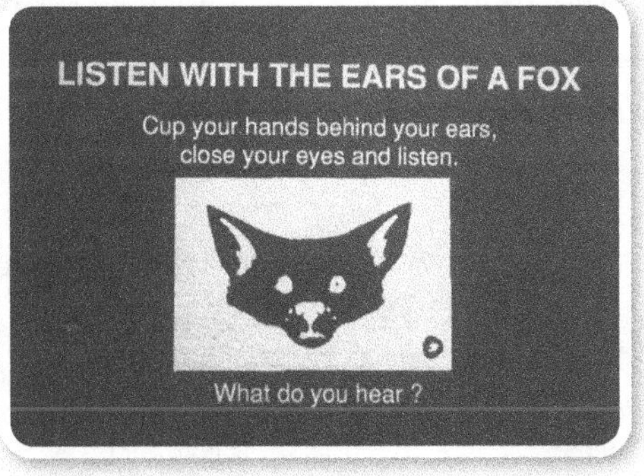

Although absorbing the trail with all five senses might cause the rush of traffic from the nearby highway to rise in one's awareness, so will cricket chirps, songbirds, hidden wildflowers, butterflies, the coolness of the shade, the heady scent of mulch from the trail, blooming cactus, and the excited voices of young children.

Trailheads

The **main trailhead** is located behind the ***Austin Nature and Science Center*** along Nature Center Drive. **Other access points** can be found (in geographical order heading south):

- Behind the Bird Sanctuary at the ANSC (open during the Center's hours)
- At the southwest end of Nature Center Drive
- Along Clubhouse Road (see "Parking" below)

Trails

Dry Creek: Stone steps lead hikers down into the trees to a dry, rocky creek bed. If you listen carefully, you'll hear the drip of water from the cliffs above.
Closest trailhead: Main trailhead

Hill Country Trail: An easy trail that crosses the Dry Creek a few times as it winds through native trees, grasses, and flowers.
Closest trailhead: Main trailhead

Mirror Pond: One of the best places for exploring, especially in the spring when the pond is full of tadpoles, minnows, dragonflies, and frogs.
Closest trailhead: Bird Sanctuary

Meadows Trail: Trees give way to open fields of native grasses and flowers.
Closest trailhead: Bird Sanctuary

Lookout Point: Hike up to a gorgeous view of the Austin skyline beyond Zilker Park.
Closest trailhead: Arnulfo Alfonso Way

Zp
Zilker Park

LOCATION Behind the Nature and Science Center at 301 Nature Center Dr.

PARKING Park in the lot under the Mopac Expy./Loop 1 bridge on Stratford Dr. Cross the street and head up the hill to the Austin Nature and Science Center. Two trailheads lie directly behind the Center along Nature Center Dr. Another can be found through the Bird Sanctuary on the grounds.

Parking is also available at the picnic area along Rollingwood Dr. Directly across the street from the picnic tables, Arnulfo Alfonso Way will lead you to the trailhead for Lookout Point that connects to the other trails below.

ADMISSION Free

Zilker Park

A map of Zilker Park can be found on pages 176-177. Detailed entries are included in this guide for each of the following locations within the park:

Ann and Roy Butler Hike and Bike Trail at Lady Bird Lake

Austin Nature and Science Center

Barton Springs Pool

Lou Neff Point

Splash! Exhibit

Umlauf Sculpture Garden

Zilker Botanical Gardens

Zilker Eagle

Zilker Nature Preserve and Hiking Trails

Zilker Park Boat Rentals

Zilker Park Playscape

Annual Events

- *Austin City Limits Festival*
- *Austin Trail of Lights*
- *Beverly S. Sheffield Zilker Hillside Theater*
- *Zilker Holiday Tree*
- *Zilker Kite Festival*

Zilker Park, located on 350 acres just south of downtown, serves as a hub for a variety of family-friendly activities and events year-round. The park contains a botanical garden, sculpture garden, playscape, soccer fields, nature center, educational water exhibit, disc golf course, hillside theater, miniature train, canoe and kayak rentals, and one of Austin's most treasured spots, ***Barton Springs Pool***. The park backs up to the Hike and Bike Trail to the northeast and the ***Barton Creek Greenbelt*** to the south, making it feel even larger.

If you are simply looking for a good place to wander with the kids, head to the playscape area. From here, you can ride the train, have a picnic, watch swimmers plunge into Barton Springs from the diving board, or visit the ***Splash! Exhibit***.

Zilker Park

LOCATION 2100 Barton Springs Rd.

WEBSITE www.austintexas.gov/department/zilker-metropolitan-park

HOURS Daily, 5AM–10PM

ADMISSION Free. Metered parking on weekends and for special events.

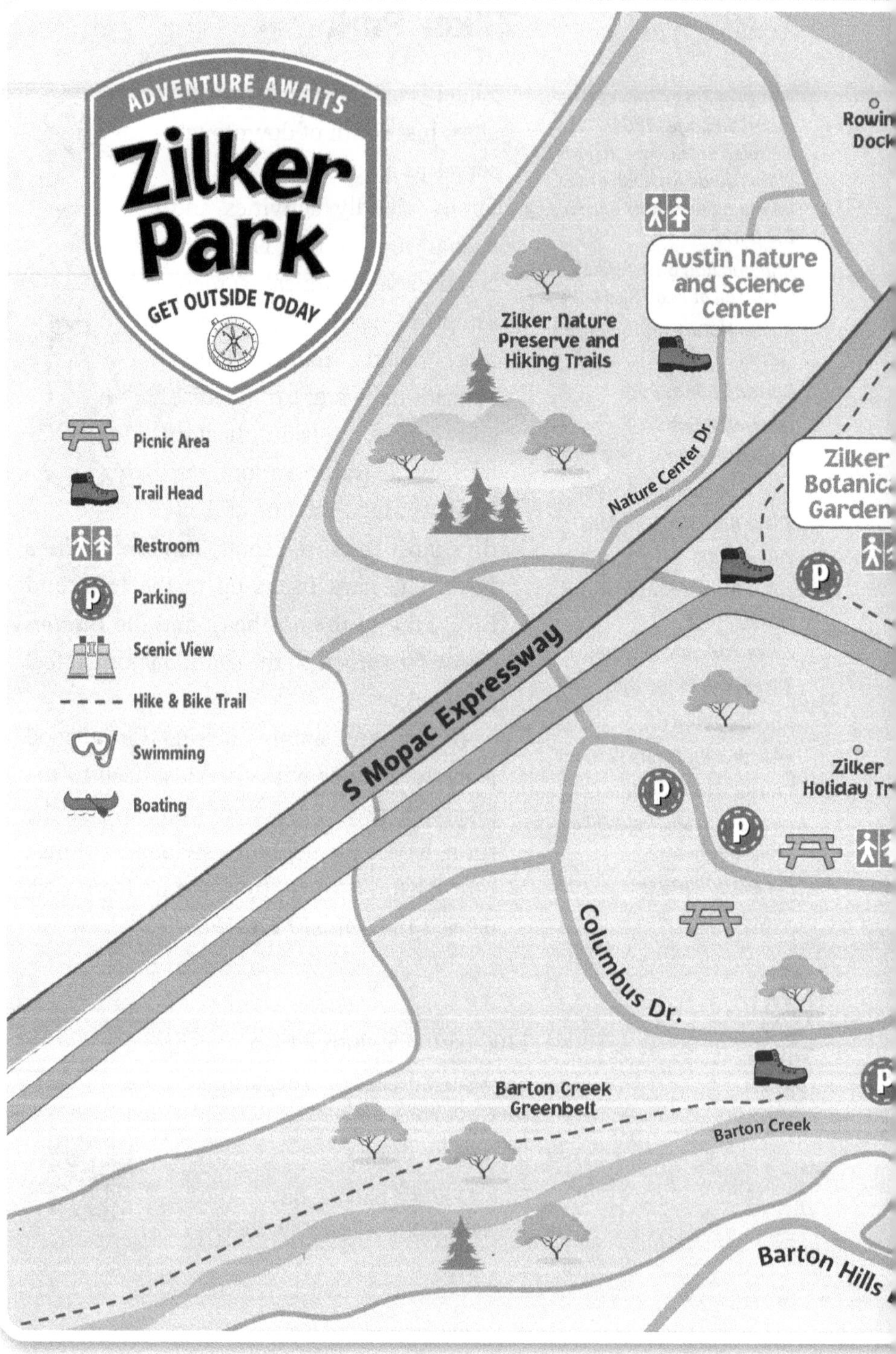
ADVENTURE AWAITS
Zilker Park
GET OUTSIDE TODAY
Picnic Area
Trail Head
Restroom
Parking
Scenic View
Hike & Bike Trail
Swimming
Boating
Zilker Nature Preserve and Hiking Trails
Austin Nature and Science Center
Nature Center Dr.
S Mopac Expressway
Columbus Dr.
Barton Creek Greenbelt
Barton Creek
Barton Hills

Lady Bird Lake
Texas Rowing Center
W Cesar Chavez Street
Lou Neff Rd.
Lou Neff Point
Rock Island
Stratford Dr.
Andrew Zilker Rd.
Playscape
Zilker Eagle
Zilker Boat Rentals
Barton Springs Road
Bridge
Splash! Exhibit
Barton Springs Pool
Robert E. Lee Road
Umlauf Sculpture Garden
© 2014 Stomping Grounds Press
www.ExploringAustinwithKids.com

Zilker Park Boat Rentals

This small wooden boathouse that sits along the trail just below Barton Springs Pool rents canoes, kayaks, and stand-up paddleboards. The water is refreshingly chilly, with water circulating from nearby springs, and it's a fine spot for putting in. Head downstream with turtles, ducks, swans, and fellow boaters to cross under two bridges on your way from Barton Creek to Lady Bird Lake. Where the creek and lake meet, you'll find a great view of downtown.

While one hour rentals—with canoes fitting two adults and two small children—are typically long enough for most families, if you'd like to go longer or have a bigger group, check the website for "two for one" coupons. You can rent a locker, if needed, or pack a waterproof bag to keep things dry. Bring a photo ID and credit card for deposit. And as the attendants advise, "Don't rock the boat!"

Zilker Park

LOCATION 2101 Andrew Zilker Rd.
below Barton Springs Pool
(Take the steps near the Zilker playscape down to the creek. The trail at the bottom leads to the boat rentals.)

PARKING Parking lots are available in Zilker Park with metered parking on weekends and for special events.

WEBSITE www.zilkerboats.com

PHONE (512) 478-3852

HOURS Daily, 9AM – dusk

ADMISSION $21/hour
$57/day

Zilker Park Playscape

Featuring an old fire truck for playing in, a music area with xylophones, a sand pile, concrete sculptures for climbing on, swings, and a large playscape, this playground is a kid's paradise and one of the larger ones in Austin. The train tracks for the ***Zilker Eagle*** divide the area in half. One of the most popular spots is on a bridge over the tracks, where children wave to passengers on the train as it runs beneath them. While the layout of the playground can create quite a challenging obstacle course for parents trying to keep up with everyone, it's a fun one for children of all ages.

Zp

Zilker Park

LOCATION 2100 Barton Springs Rd.

PARKING Adjacent parking lots are available in Zilker Park. Metered parking on weekends and for special events.

WEBSITE www.austintexas.gov/department/zilker-metropolitan-park

ADMISSION Free

Places to Eat

Austin's most delicious, relaxed, family-friendly dining

Amy's Ice Creams

I scream, you scream, we all scream for ICE CREAM! Amy's is especially worth screaming about for several reasons:

For one, it's yummy! Old standbys like Belgian Chocolate, Dark Chocolate, Mexican Vanilla, and Sweet Cream are scooped up alongside a rotating selection of creative flavors like Oatmeal Raisin Cookie, S'mores, Mint Ice Cream Sandwich, Cheesecake, Strawberry Lime Pie, or Peanut Butter Honey Sandwich. And forget "toppings." At Amy's you choose from a long list of "crush'ns" that are chopped, crushed, and mixed into your slab of ice cream by hand to create a flavor of your own delicious devising. There are fruit ices, yogurts, milkshakes, and smoothies too.

Two, it's an experience. Amy's hires wacky, fun-loving staff.

And three, it's local. Amy opened her first shop on 35th Street and Guadalupe in 1984 and shops have been popping up all over town (and Texas) ever since.

If you want to make your trip to Amy's even more of an experience, visit the Arboretum location where you can wander down a short path to play on giant marble cows beneath the trees. Or continue on to take a trail down to the pond to feed the geese and ducks.

Three other fun locations are paired with ***Phil's Icehouse*** that makes great burgers and serves local draft beer. These not only have cows to play on but playscapes so kids can burn off sugar highs.

Multiple Locations

LOCATION	Throughout the city
WEBSITE	www.amysicecreams.com
HOURS	Vary by location

Big Top Candy Shop

Step into this narrow slip of a store, seemingly miles long to children as their eyes pop at the ceiling-to-floor candy selections, and the phrase "like a kid in a candy shop" is taken to a whole new level. The choices of familiar treats, unheard of delectables, and sweets from decades past seem endless: huge lollipops, Payday bars, 5th Avenue, Oh Henry!, candy by the piece, fine chocolates, chocolate covered insects, hard candy, salty candy, bulk candy, gummy anything you can imagine, truffles, licorice, bins of jelly beans, jaw breakers, bubblegum, and Wonka bars. They have it all, including an old-fashioned soda fountain where soda jerks whip up milkshakes, malts, and sodas. Curiosity and delight abound for children and adults alike as they wander the length of this circus-themed shop to peruse candy bins beneath brightly colored posters that feature acts like "Snake Boy" and "Voodoo Witch" alongside brass instruments and steampunk art. It's a museum of goodness.

South Austin

LOCATION 1706 S. Congress Ave.

PARKING Curb parking along Congress Ave. and neighboring streets (watch for Resident Only Parking signs), or the parking garage behind Guerro's Restaurant at Congress Ave. and Elizabeth St.

WEBSITE www.bigtopcandyshop.com

PHONE (512) 462-2220

HOURS **"Open 'til they close," roughly:**

Sunday – Thursday	11AM – 7PM
Friday	11AM – 9PM
Saturday	10AM – 9PM

Casey's New Orleans Snowballs

This family-run business from New Orleans operates out of a little white house with orders placed through the front porch windows. Friendly staff scoop up the softest, fluffiest ice, then use a straw to punch tunnels in it for the hand-mixed syrups to fully saturate the snowball. This extra ice is often flicked on the heads of eagerly awaiting young ones hoping for it to "snow!" These treats come in a range of sizes, from junior flattop to jumbo. In addition to traditional flavors made in-house with pure cane sugar, Casey's also offers sugar-free syrups, juice balls made of 100 % fruit juice, special toppings, and cream flavors that melt in your mouth.

North Central

DATES End of March through early fall

LOCATION 808 E. 51st St. (at the intersection of Airport Blvd.)

WEBSITE www.caseys-snowballs.com

HOURS Daily, noon – 9PM

Central Market—North Lamar location

This cafe is popular among families for its playscape beneath large oak trees and ample outdoor seating that extends from the cafe to the back deck patio near the playground. The restaurant dishes up good, healthy food, tasty drinks, and gelato for dessert. On weekend evenings, early live music sets play on the patio during dinnertime, with plenty of dancing room. The cafe can get crowded

on nice days and evenings, but Central Park directly behind it offers additional open space for picnicking, running off energy, watching ducks, climbing trees, or wandering the ¾-mile trail that loops around the pond. Check the online calendar for special events and free live music (typically performed on the weekends).

North Central

LOCATION 4001 N. Lamar Blvd.
WEBSITE www.centralmarket.com
PHONE (512) 206-1000
CAFE HOURS Daily, 8AM–10PM

Doc's Backyard

Despite its location in a strip mall, large garage doors open onto an expansive outdoor picnic area and pavilion that slope to two playscapes, making it a favorite among families. The playground rests beneath a grove of oak trees backed by ranchland that provides a scenic backdrop for watching the kids play. The playground is good for all ages with a separate, smaller corralled area with a playhouse for toddlers. The menu features American fare with some Mexican flair, and a full bar is available with a selection of Texas craft beers. Kids can order staples like mini-burgers, mini-hot dogs, and crustless PB&J sandwiches.

South Austin

LOCATION 5207 Brodie Ln.

WEBSITE www.eatdrinkdocs.com

PHONE (512) 892-5200

HOURS
Monday – Thursday 11AM – 11PM
Friday – Saturday 11AM – midnight
Sunday 11AM – 11PM

Easy Tiger

This bakery and beer garden serves a great weekend brunch and tasty breakfast pastries. For lunch or dinner, try their salads, soups, sandwiches, and burgers with a range of fresh-baked breads. A kids' menu contains all the classics from hot dogs and hamburgers to grilled cheese and chicken tenders.

While adults may enjoy the second-story porch bar where you can catch a good sunset, kids will like the Little Tiger Den just across the drive from the restaurant's main entrance. The enclosed, outdoor area provides young children a space to play within eyesight of picnic tables nestled under string lights and oak trees. Kids can climb a tunnel lined with turf, play yard games, and decorate chalkboard panels that line the metal fence, set against a backdrop of green space.

South Austin

LOCATION 3508 S. Lamar Blvd.

WEBSITE www.easytigerusa.com/location/south

PHONE (512) 964-8229

HOURS Sunday – Thursday 7AM – 9:30PM
Friday – Saturday 7AM – 10:30PM

Flores Mexican Restaurant

This restaurant serves up a good mix of authentic Mexican dishes and traditional Tex-Mex. Although there isn't a separate kids menu, smaller portions can be created from the extensive sides section. (Burgers and chicken fingers are also an option.) Mexican-food lovers will appreciate the variety of taco plates, enchilada specials, and seafood dishes as well as the fresh tortillas made in-house. The restaurant's décor reflects a similar Mexican-Texan blend. Brightly painted walls, decorative tile, and large wooden doors that open onto spacious dining rooms blend easily with the outdoor wooden porches and patio areas. A large, playscape surrounded by oak trees and picnic tables create space for an easy family dinner.

Multiple Locations

LOCATION AND PHONE

North
Four Points
8300 N. FM 620
(512) 996-9636

South
South Austin
4625 William Cannon Dr.
(512) 892-4845

West of Town
Dripping Springs
2440 E. Hwy. 290
(512) 858-2221

Lakeway
2127 Lohmans Crossing Rd.
(512) 263-9546

HOURS

Tuesday – Thursday	11AM – 9PM
Friday	11AM – 10PM
Saturday – Sunday	11AM – 9PM
Monday	closed

WEBSITE www.floresmexican.com

Hat Creek Burger Company

The focus on community is clear at this homegrown fast food chain, from the fun playgrounds that serve as focal points for families to gather to the locally sourced beef, veggies, and craft beers. Fundraising nights for area schools, weekend pajama parties, and birthday celebrations are a regular occurrence as well.

This burger restaurant offers a range of choices beyond the standard beef burger too. Their varied menu includes breakfast options, salads, chicken burgers, or vegetarian and gluten-free entrees. Kids can add sides of fruit cups or apple pouches to their meals before hitting the playground to burn off more energy. For dessert, try specialty milk shakes like the Birthday Cake with sprinkles or Peanut Butter Cup, or choose toppings and create your own unique concoction.

Multiple Locations

LOCATION AND PHONE

North

Domain
3210 Esperanza Crossing
(512) 838-6224
Daily, 11AM – 9PM

Round Rock
3700 E. Palm Valley Blvd.
(512) 428-6164

North Central

Burnet Road
5400 Burnet Road
(512) 452-2025
Daily, 10:30AM – 8PM

West

West Lake
5902 Bee Cave Rd.
(512) 296-2151

West of Town

Dripping Springs
166 Hargraves Dr.
(512) 432-0161

Lakeway
1602 Ranch Rd. 620 S
(512) 712-5968

HOURS *Unless otherwise noted*

Monday – Thursday	7AM – 9PM
Friday	7AM – 9PM
Saturday	8AM – 9:30PM
Sunday	8AM – 9PM

WEBSITE www.hatcreekburgers.com

Home Slice Pizza

This classic New York style pizza joint serves delicious thin crust pies, Italian sub sandwiches, calzones, and salads. The hip restaurant located in the heart of SoCo stays busy! So go early on a weekday to avoid a long wait, or simply be prepared to order some drinks and hang out. To keep up with demand, the owners also opened a "takeout and slices only" shop next door. So if hungry tummies can't wait, order a pie to go or grab some slices at More Home Slice. If you're in the north Central neighborhood, visit Home Slice North Loop with its unique play area of rolling turf for the kids.

Multiple Locations

LOCATION, PHONE, AND HOURS

South

Home Slice Pizza
1415 S. Congress Ave.
(512) 444-7437
Mon, Wed, Thurs 11AM–11PM
Friday–Saturday 11AM–midnight
Sunday 11AM–11PM
Tuesday closed

More Home Slice
1421 S. Congress Ave.
(512) 444-7437
Sunday–Thursday 11AM–11PM
Friday–Saturday 11AM–midnight

North Central

Home Slice Pizza
501 E. 53rd St.
(512) 707-7437
Sunday–Thursday 11AM–11PM
Friday–Saturday 11AM–midnight

WEBSITE www.homeslicepizza.com

Jester King Brewery

Barn-style buildings filled with long picnic tables overhung by dangling chandeliers, delicious pizza pies, local beer taps, and scenic Hill Country surroundings make this brewery a weekend destination. Jester King offers regular tours and tastings from its sustainably-focused brewery, and you can sit and sip your brew at shaded outdoor tables that offer an expansive view of the property. To see even more, hop on the two-mile nature trail that loops through Hill Country terrain. Be back to catch the sunset view from the brewery.

Relaxed outdoor seating surrounds both the barn and the restaurant that serves garlic knots, salads, wood-fired pizzas, and other local brews. If you plan to eat, go early as lines can occasionally get long. Opposite the outdoor restaurant, the barn opens to fields and a playground, ideal spots for kids to play and explore within eyeshot. Another favorite spot is the goat barn up the hill.

Vista Brewing in Driftwood, just a bit farther south, is another great family-friendly brewpub.

West Austin

LOCATION 13187 Fitzhugh Rd.
From Hwy. 290 West, the entrance is 2.9 miles down Fitzhugh Rd. and can be easy to miss. Start looking for it on your left after passing Long Branch Valley on the right and Ceres Park on your left.

WEBSITE www.jesterkingbrewery.com

HOURS
Thursday – Friday 2PM – 9PM
Saturday 11AM – 9PM
Sunday 11AM – 8PM
Monday – Wednesday closed
Food trucks and pizzeria close an hour earlier.

Kerbey Lane Café

Kerbey Lane is one of those places where everyone can find something they like and know it will be yummy. They make dishes with fresh local ingredients so good they inspire seasonal menus. With creative pancake specials, Kerbey Lane shines when it comes to breakfast, and they serve it all hours. The café is also known for its vegetarian, vegan, and gluten-free menus. Chefs cook up a wide array of salads, sandwiches, enchiladas, burgers, and soups, with a nice twist on traditional favorites. While the original restaurant can be found on Kerbey Lane, other locations have popped up across the city, all with a relaxed atmosphere. Expect a wait for Sunday brunch. Tuesday nights, kids eat free.

Multiple Locations

LOCATION, PHONE, AND HOURS

North Austin

13435 Hwy. 183
(512) 258-7757
Daily, 7 AM – 10 PM

North Central

3704 Kerbey Ln.
(512) 451-1436
Daily, 7 AM – 10 PM

2200 Aldrich St.
(512) 879-2818
Daily, 7 AM – 10 PM

University of Texas Area

2606 Guadalupe St.
(512) 477-5717
Daily, 7 AM – midnight

West

701 S. Capital of TX Hwy.
(512) 879-2820
Daily, 7 AM – 10 PM

South

3003 S. Lamar Blvd.
(512) 445-4451
Sunday – Thursday
7 AM – 10 PM
Friday – Saturday
7 AM – midnight

4301 W. William Cannon Dr.
(512) 899-1500
Sunday – Thursday
7 AM – 10 PM
Friday – Saturday
7 AM – midnight

WEBSITE www.kerbeylanecafe.com

Mandola's Italian Kitchen

The lively atmosphere at Mandola's can make it feel as if you're dining with a big Italian family. Diners are seated amidst Italian market décor, wines, and goods while treated to the smells of fresh pasta and sauces simmering in the open kitchen. Tables are closely spaced to maximize the number of diners and minimize waits. Order at the counter, then grab a table. Small children can even snag a kid-sized table of their own! Outdoor seating provides another option, with a playground adjacent or nearby, depending on the location.

Waiters are quick to bring bread for snacking while you wait for your meal. The menu has everything from pizza and lasagna to gnocchi and eggplant parmigiana. Kid meals come with a drink and a scoop of gelato for dessert. Adults may be tempted to check out dessert options as well. In addition to gelato flavors ranging from cinnamon and coconut to chocolate and tiramisu, the dessert cases contain delicious cakes, Italian pastries, cannoli, and cookies.

Multiple Locations

LOCATION, PHONE, AND HOURS

North

Cedar Park
12100 W. Parmer Ln. Ste. 200
(512) 879-1450
Sunday – Thursday
11AM – 9PM
Friday – Saturday
11AM – 10PM

North Central

The Triangle
4700 W. Guadalupe St.
(512) 419-9700
Monday – Saturday
11AM – 10PM
Sunday
11AM – 9PM

West of Town

Bee Cave
12815 Shops Pkwy.
(512) 600-8500
Daily, 11AM – 9PM

South

Arbor Trails
4301 W. William Cannon Dr.
(512) 524-2222
Daily, 11AM – 9PM

WEBSITE www.mandolas.com

Places to Eat

Matt's El Rancho

With its mission-style architecture, handsomely engraved front doors, and outdoor courtyard, entering Matt's feels like walking into old Mexico. The "King of Mexican Food," Matt Martinez, and his family have been in business since 1952 serving Tex-Mex favorites like enchilada plates, carne guisada, tacos, fajitas, and grilled sirloin steaks as well as more traditional Mexican seafood dishes. The children's menu offers a range of options too, from fajitas, grilled veggies on Spanish rice, or broccoli with a side of queso to cheese quesadillas, chicken strips, or burgers. Kids can watch the grill and tortillas being made from scratch behind large glass windows near the kitchen. The outdoor courtyard also provides a family-friendly place to eat, relaxing for parents and entertaining for kids with its fountain filled with fish. Go early to avoid long waits.

Long wait at Matt's? There's no shortage of Mexican food in this area! Try Curra's, El Mercado, Fresa's, Güero's, Maudie's, or Torchy's Tacos—all with outdoor patios.

South Austin

LOCATION 2613 S. Lamar Blvd.
WEBSITE www.mattselrancho.com
PHONE (512) 462-9333
HOURS

Mon, Wed, Thurs	11AM–10PM
Friday–Saturday	11AM–11PM
Sunday	11AM–9PM
Tuesday	closed

Places to Eat

Meanwhile Brewing Company

This local brewery seems designed with families and community in mind. The first hint is the large, enclosed soccer field near the front entrance. Next, you'll find an ice cream truck fronting a food court, a layout that seems to imply, "Eat dessert first!" Drinks can be ordered in the brewery or from the porch window.

Behind the brewery, a slew of picnic tables and wooden Adirondack chairs fill what feels like a big backyard. An expansive, hand-built playground shaded by cedar trees provides plenty of room to play. On weekends, don't be surprised to be greeted by children's birthday parties during the day and by live music at night. Community-oriented fairs and events are regularly held as well.

South Austin

LOCATION 3901 Promontory Point Dr.

WEBSITE www.meanwhilebeer.com

PHONE (512) 308-3659

HOURS

Monday – Wednesday	8AM – 10PM
Thursday – Friday	8AM – 11PM
Saturday	9AM – 11PM
Sunday	9AM – 9PM

Phil's Ice House

This popular family-friendly restaurant serves up tasty burgers (named after funky local neighborhoods), sweet potato fries, and draft beer. A children's menu is also available. The original location on Burnet Road was converted from the old Allandale post office and gas station. On nice days, the garage doors in the dining area open and seating flows out to the picnic tables near the playscape. At the location on South Lamar Boulevard, the outdoor seating and play area sit beneath the shade of big oak trees. The newest Phil's in North Austin also features live feed from its skydiving neighbor, iFLY. To top it all off, these restaurants are connected to ***Amy's Ice Creams***, so save room for dessert!

Multiple Locations

LOCATION, PHONE, AND HOURS

North
13265 US Hwy. 183 N
(512) 257-8750
Sunday – Thursday
11AM – 9PM
Friday – Saturday
11AM – 10PM

North Central
5620 Burnet Rd.
(512) 524-1212
Sunday – Thursday
11AM – 9PM
Friday – Saturday
11AM – 10PM

South
2901 S. Lamar Blvd.
(512) 707-8704
Sunday – Thursday
11AM – 9PM
Friday – Saturday
11AM – 10PM

WEBSITE www.philsicehouse.com

Places to Eat

Salt Lick

Delicious and locally famous, the Salt Lick is off the beaten path, located south of Austin in Driftwood, but the drive out to a scenic setting merely adds to the experience. The restaurant, which started in 1967 with just a handcrafted barbecue pit, has grown to include rustic buildings filled with rows of long wooden picnic tables, relaxing outdoor patios, an adjacent vineyard, wine cellars, and a large playground area for children to play when waits are long. Grab a beer or glass of wine from Salt Lick Cellars, or bring your own. The simple menu covers all the staples with meat served by the pound, on a plate piled high with sides, in a Texas-sized sandwich, or family style. Small plates are available for kids. Top it off with pie or cobbler à la mode. Cash only.

South Austin

LOCATION	18300 FM 1826, Driftwood
WEBSITE	www.saltlickbbq.com/driftwood
PHONE	(512) 858-4959
HOURS	Sunday – Thursday 11AM – 9PM Friday – Saturday 11AM – 10PM

Sandy's Hamburgers

Around since 1946, Sandy's is a classic burger joint with a simple menu of burgers, fries, and hot dogs for meals, but it only takes a glance at their giant ice cream cone-shaped sign to know what customers really come for — the desserts. A full half of the menu is dedicated to drinks, floats, shakes, malts, and frozen custard. Visitors can sit on the front bench to lick their soft-serve cones on a sunny day, or grab an outdoor table behind the small building.

South Austin

LOCATION 603 Barton Springs Rd.
WEBSITE www.sandysaustin.com
PHONE (512) 478-6322
HOURS Daily, 10AM–10:30PM

Ski Shores Café

Ski Shores has a long history of providing relaxed lakeside dining with its family-friendly roots dating back to 1954. The menu is fairly simple with burgers, tacos, salads, fish baskets, and a variety of drinks. A children's menu offers smaller fare suited to children's tastes. The appeal is the location. Drive out or boat up to eat at shaded picnic tables that snake along the shore of Lake Austin and watch swans, ducks, and boats pass by. Seating can also be found beneath tall trees next to an enclosed area with lawn games and a pickle ball court. Check social media for their Live on the Lake music series and season-themed special events.

For lakeside dining closer to town, hit up the Hula Hut on Lake Austin.

West Austin

LOCATION 2905 Pearce Rd.

WEBSITE www.skishorescafe.com

PHONE (512) 572-2997

HOURS Hours change with the seasons and weather. Call or check online for the latest.

Sno-Beach

Sno-Beach is one of Austin's most popular sno-cone stands, and one of the city's first food trailers. It has been providing Austinites this summertime staple for over twenty years. The location is part of the appeal. To cool off inside and out, many combine a trip with a plunge in ***Barton Springs Pool***. Customers line up to choose from a long list of traditional flavors as well as a few sugar-free choices, with the option to top it off with caramel or cream. In the face of a changing Austin and due to the transitory nature of food trailers, there's always the chance that Sno-Beach could be on the move, so check the address before you go. But this sweet stand will very likely stick around.

South Austin

DATES March – October
LOCATION 412 Sterzing St.
WEBSITE www.snobeachatx.com
HOURS Summer, noon – sundown
Off season, 2PM – 7PM

Sugar Mama's Bakeshop

You have never had cupcakes *this* good: buttery vanilla cupcakes topped with dollops of buttercream frosting and sprinkled with sugar, moist red velvet cupcakes, carrot cupcakes, vegan mint chocolate cupcakes, chocolate cupcakes with chocolate frosting.... This bakery whips up deliciously decadent desserts, made from scratch each morning. Decked out in 50's retro style, the décor ties in perfectly with the names of the cupcakes, from the Marilyn Monroe to the James Brown or Elvis. Daily specials complement the handful of regular flavors, always with gluten-free or vegan options. Displayed beside the cupcakes are a variety of mini-pies, cookies, and bars to pick from too. The size is good for kids, big and fancy enough to be a special treat without overwhelming their tummies.

South Austin

LOCATION 1905 S. First St.

PARKING A small lot is located directly behind the building.

WEBSITE www.sugarmamasbakeshop.com

PHONE (512) 448-3727

HOURS Tuesday – Saturday 10AM – 7PM
Sunday – Monday closed

Waterloo Ice House

Waterloo Ice House has been around since the 1970s and maintains a laid back, old Austin vibe. Offering casual Texas dining, the rustic-themed locations below feature tall ceilings, big windows, and playgrounds for the kids. Open for breakfast, lunch, and dinner, dishes are Southern inspired with Tex-Mex flair thrown in for good measure. Choose from tacos, burgers, sandwiches, and platters. Kids' menus offer tasty classics with a few twists like Texas tortilla catfish and half-baked cookies smothered in ice cream and chocolate syrup.

Multiple Locations

KID-FRIENDLY LOCATIONS, PHONE, AND HOURS

West

6203 N. Capital of Texas Hwy.
(512) 418-9700

Monday – Wednesday
7AM – 10PM

Thursday – Friday
7AM – 11PM

Saturday
8AM – 11PM

Sunday
8AM – 10PM

South

9600 Escarpment Blvd.
(512) 301-1007

Monday – Wednesday
7AM – 10PM

Thursday – Friday
7AM – 11PM

Saturday
8AM – 11PM

Sunday
8AM – 10PM

9600 S. 1-35
(512) 292-7900

Thursday – Saturday
8AM – 11PM

Sunday – Wedesday
8AM – 10PM

WEBSITE www.waterlooicehouse.com

Whole Foods Rooftop

There is a little-known playground atop the roof of the flagship downtown Whole Foods Market. Pack up snacks or a meal from the store and take the outdoor stairs or the elevator up a level. Shaded tables sit adjacent to a small playground (best for young children) where families can dine, play, and enjoy the rooftop view. Check the store calendar for rooftop events that have included Shakespearean plays, movies, live music, and ice skating.

Downtown Austin

LOCATION 525 N. Lamar Blvd.
(corner of 6th St. and Lamar Blvd.)

WEBSITE www.wholefoods.com/stores/lamar

PHONE (512) 542-2200

HOURS Daily, 7AM–10PM

[illegible]

Annual Events

03 Events Calendar Jan–June

01 January

02 February

- Juggle Fest

03 March

- South by Southwest Festival (SXSW)
- Rodeo Austin
- Rock the Park
- Honk!TX Festival

04 April

- Honk!TX Festival
- Zilker Kite Festival
- Squirrel Fest
- Camp Mabry Living History Weekend
- Rock the Park
- Austin Dragon Boat Festival and Race
- Eeyore's Birthday Party

05 May

- Rock the Park
- Shakespeare in the Park

06 June

- Nature Nights at the Lady Bird Johnson Wildflower Center
- Austin Symphony Orchestra's Tuneful Tales
- Rock the Park

Events Calendar July – Dec

07 July

- Austin Symphony Orchestra's Tuneful Tales
- Beverly S. Sheffield Zilker Hillside Theater Summer Musial

08 August

- Beverly S. Sheffield Zilker Hillside Theater Summer Musial

09 September

- Austin Museum Day
- Touch-A-Truck
- Rock the Park

10 October

- Austin City Limits Festival
- Boo at the Zoo
- Crowe's Nest Farm Fall Family Fun Fest
- Rock the Park
- Día de los Muertos Viva La Vida Fest

11 November

- Texas Book Festival
- Rock the Park
- Waterloo Greenway Creek Show

12 December

- Holiday Sing-Along & Downtown Stroll
- Austin Trail of Lights
- Zilker Holiday Tree
- Luminations at Lady Bird Johnson Wildflower Center
- Christmas Lights on 37th Street

Juggle Fest

Sitting in an auditorium with a crowd of giggling children enthralled by juggling balls, rings and cones, circus acts, and pure zaniness is not a bad way to spend the evening. The Public Show put on by the Texas Juggling Society as part of its three-day Juggle Fest features performers from all over the country and is filled with silliness, fun, and magic. Hearkening back to an older time in entertainment, it's perfect theater for kids. For those with an aspiring juggler in the family, purchase a wristband for the entire weekend event of workshops, games, and insider tips.

South Austin

DATE Weekend in February or March

TIME Workshops are held Friday evening and all day Saturday and Sunday. The Public Show happens Saturday night (typically 7:30PM). See website for schedule of events.

LOCATION Check website

WEBSITE www.juggling.place.org/jugglefest

ADMISSION $20 Ticket for Public Show for ages 6 and up

South by Southwest Festival (SXSW)

Originally a weekend-long music festival to showcase local talent, South by Southwest quickly attracted national and international attention. Now bands and fans come from all over, and the week-long music festival fills the city with music—in venues, parking lots, parks, neighborhood backyards, food trailer parks, and rooftops. And there's more than just music. Continuing to expand, SXSW now encompasses a film, comedy, and interactive festival that span nearly two weeks.

While there are wristbands and detailed schedules of events for professionals and music or film aficionados, for families looking to experience good music and interactive fun on the cheap, unofficial events are held throughout the city. The key can be knowing the right resources to consult and which direction to head out.

SXSW Music

For those who simply like to happen upon good music while wandering, hit up South Congress Avenue. Bands play up and down this trendy, funky stretch, dubbed SoCo. Meander between the outdoor stage at Jo's Coffee (South x San Jose) on the north end, and explore music-filled alleyways and shops all the way to Magnolia Café at the south end of the strip. Each year, you can catch free shows at the Outdoor Stage at Lady Bird Lake. Find lineups and other happenings under the Free Events menu on the SXSW website.

Check these online sites for schedules of kid-friendly and kid-focused events:

Austin.com	www.austin.com
Do 512 Family	www.do512family.com
365 Things to Do	www.365thingsaustin.com/family
The Austin Chronicle	www.austinchronicle.com for full listings of events

Multiple Locations

DATE Mid-March

WEBSITE www.sxsw.com

ADMISSION Check website for admission fees, wristbands, and free events

Rodeo Austin

The Star of Texas Fair and Rodeo is a tradition all ages will enjoy. Families can wander the Fairgrounds in a relaxed atmosphere while listening to country music (often live) and check out Ol' McDonald's Barn where cattle, pigs, sheep, turkeys, and rabbits wait to be shown and baby chicks totter about in the Hatchery. In nearby Kidstown, young cowboys and cowgirls can saddle up on ponies, visit the petting zoo, or watch milking demonstrations. Shows are often held around the grounds, from puppets to pig racing to Wild West shows. For additional thrills, visit the Carnival, a large expanse of rides where kids can roam for hours riding miniature trains, slides, roller coasters, and ferris wheels. The pro-rodeo events (including steer wrestling, barrel racing, bull riding, clowns, and more) begin each evening and conclude with a live concert in the Luedecke Arena. Food and drinks are available from a variety of vendors.

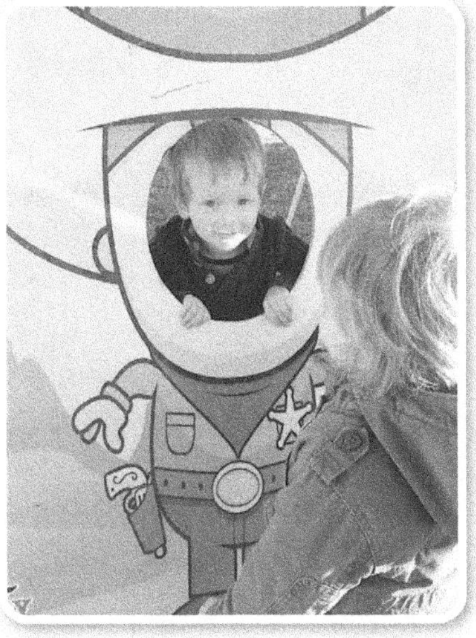

East Austin

DATES Two weeks, mid-March

TIME Varies by day (check the online schedule). The Fairgrounds and Carnival open early. Rodeo events and concert begin in the evening.

LOCATION Travis County Expo Center at 9100 Decker Lake Rd.

Website www.rodeoaustin.com

Phone (512) 919-3000

Admission **Parking fee:** $15

Fairgrounds only:
Free children under 3
$5 children ages 3-12
$10 teens and adults

Carnival:
$20-40 adult unlimited ride wristband

Rodeo & Concert tickets (includes Fairgrounds):
Tickets range from $30-$175 depending on seats

Rock the Park

Picnic blankets spill over the hillside that slopes down to an outdoor amphitheater where kids fill the dance floor, enthusiastically jamming to the music. With Mueller Lake as a backdrop, it's a nice, family-friendly way to spend the evening celebrating community and live music. The series runs throughout the spring and fall, with one show per month from March to June, and from September to November. Favorite children's performers open the concerts, followed by musical performances by local bands. All shows are kid-friendly, and the event wraps up by dark.

Arrive early to secure your space with a blanket. Hit up the food trucks or get takeout from a nearby restaurant for a picnic. Then head to the playground until the show starts.

North Central

DATE Friday evenings

TIME 6:30PM – 8:30PM

LOCATION Mueller Lake Park, 4550 Mueller Blvd.

PARKING McBee Parking Garage or metered street parking around the park.

WEBSITE www.kutx.org/live-events/kutx-events/rock-the-park

ADMISSION Free

Honk!TX Festival

Community-focused, outdoors, funky, and fun, HONK! revives the weird, old, Austin music scene in vibrant force. The three-day nonprofit festival is free and uniquely mobile. To reach as many fans as possible, the event moves across town over the span of the weekend. Shows typically begin at an outdoor venue on Friday evening, followed by daytime Saturday performances in Central Austin green space, ending with a fantastical parade of floats, costumes, and bands that march, pedal, and stilt-walk their way through East Austin to a city park for Sunday afternoon performances.

Bands include local favorites as well as national and international acts. The lineup represents a broad range of musical styles, infusing a laid-back Austin style with a bit of Carnival energy and New Orleans spirit, always with lots of brass and lots of band members, making it lots of fun.

You don't need much to enjoy this festival. Pack hats, snacks, a blanket, or chairs. The venues tend to be family-friendly with playgrounds and green space to roam.

Multiple Locations

DATE Weekend in late March or early April

TIME & LOCATION Check the website for the full schedule of events and locations.

WEBSITE http://www.honktx.org

ADMISSION Free

Zilker Kite Festival

This festival has celebrated the simple joy of springtime kite flying since 1929, making Austin home to one of the longest running kite festivals in the country. ***Zilker Park*** is dedicated to kite flyers and picnickers on this day. Contests for the highest flying, smallest, steadiest, biggest, and most unusual kites are held in the competitors' field. Vendors offer food, drinks, and children's activities nearby. If you're willing to wait in line, a ride on the ***Zilker Eagle*** offers a neat view of the entire event. With attendance ranging in the thousands, it's best to arrive early. So pack a lunch, set up a blanket, and watch the largest range of kites you're likely to see all year. Or bring your own and give it a go.

Zilker Park

DATE: Sunday in April (check website for date)

TIME: 10AM–5PM

LOCATION: Zilker Park, 2100 Barton Springs Rd.

PARKING: Parking can be difficult, so go early or consider taking a shuttle for a minimal fee. Kids and dogs ride free. Note that Barton Springs Rd. is closed during the event.

WEBSITE: www.abckitefest.org

PHONE: (512) 448-5483

ADMISSION: Free

Squirrel Fest

Hosted by Pease Park Conservancy, this festival celebrates the recently revamped Pease Park. On any typical day, most kids would jump at the chance to visit the park's new splash pad area, wooden playground, and treehouse structure. The added festivities of Squirrel Fest just make it that much more exciting. Unlike ***Eeyore's Birthday Party***, which happens here at the end of the month, this festival is all about kids. Activities include such things as puppet shows, music classes, family yoga, and tours of fire trucks. You will also find sponsored booths, roaming bands, and lots of local vendors selling their wares. The event concludes with a family-friendly outdoor movie.

Despite the festival feel to the event, there is still plenty of space to spread out or picnic. A few food and drink vendors are on site, or pack your own picnic to enjoy a day at the park.

Univ of Texas Area

DATES	Saturday in April
TIME	4PM – 10PM
LOCATION	Pease Park, 1100 Kingsbury St.
PARKING	See www.peasepark.org/parking for transportation and parking options.
WEBSITE	www.peasepark.org/squirrel-fest
ADMISSION	Free

Camp Mabry Living History Weekend

During this annual event in honor of our military, visitors are invited to tour the extensive grounds of ***Camp Mabry*** in army vehicles, climb aboard aircrafts on display, and explore the Texas Military Forces Museum or the tanks on Artillery Row. Military men and women dressed in period uniform share history from the Civil War to present day from historically recreated military camps around the base. As part of the educational mission of the event, impressive living history demonstrations and reenactments are scheduled throughout the weekend. (Check online for the schedule of events.) Though most will leave with further appreciation for our men and women in uniform, children fascinated by all things military will be especially impressed by this event.

West Austin

DATE	Mid-April on Muster weekend
TIME	Call or check the online schedule
LOCATION	3038 W. 35th St. The public entrance to Camp Mabry is off of 35th St., just west of Mopac Expy./Loop 1. Drive half a mile past the old main gate (now barricaded), through the light at Exposition Blvd. At the bottom of the hill, just before a flashing traffic signal, turn right onto Maintenance Dr. to the gated entrance.
WEBSITE	www.texasmilitaryforcesmuseum.org
PHONE	(512) 782-5659
ADMISSION	Free

Austin Dragon Boat Festival and Race

This cultural event will captivate the attention of children and their parents as teams of rowers fly by in boats decked out like dragons during the daylong races on Lady Bird Lake. Families can watch from beneath the trees along the banks or on the docks for a closer view. Another highlight is the lineup of all-day performances by children's groups and local organizations representing a range of Asian cultures, from Hawaiian dances and Japanese Taiko drums to martial arts and Chinese dragon dances. There are plenty of booths with free children's activities and prizes. Delicious traditional foods are available at vendor booths too, healthier and tastier than typical festival fare. The event is a wonderful way to spend the morning alongside the lake while celebrating Asian cultures.

The Dragon Boat Races are sponsored by the Asian American Cultural Center. The center hosts a preschool, summer camps, adult classes, and family events all year.

South Austin

DATE Last Saturday in April

TIME Varies (check website)

LOCATION 2101 Bergman St. at Festival Beach along Lady Bird Lake

PARKING Parking lots are available along the stretch of the park as well as street parking nearby.

WEBSITE www.asianamericancc.com
www.atxdragonboat.com

ADMISSION Free

Eeyore's Birthday Party

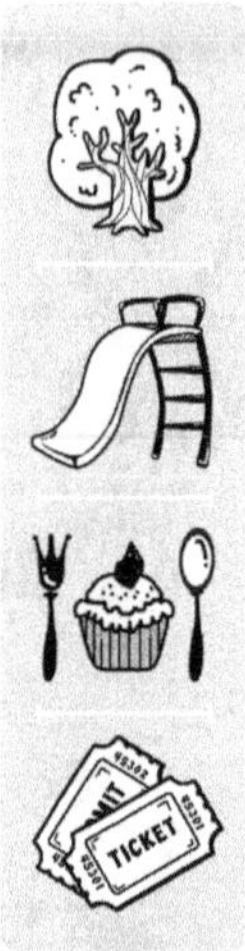

Eeyore's is a truly one-of-a-kind phenomenon. If you're on the hunt for the increasingly elusive "weird" to be found in Austin, there is no shortage at this event. Originating in the 1960s with University of Texas students celebrating the birthday of the A.A. Milne character Eeyore the donkey, the event has come to attract college students, hippies of all ages, families, and anyone with an appreciation for the fun and truly wacky. Live music plays, a drum circle beats all day, and outlandish costumes abound. If you forget yours, you can count on the face painting, temporary tattoo, and colored hair spray booths to get you festive.

It's best to get there early in the day when the Children's Area is open and the event is more family-friendly (before the crowd grows and some of the more eccentric costumes include little more than body paint). Children can head to the playground located near the free crafts and activities area, or purchase tickets to play games with prizes. Food and drink vendors are also on the grounds, as is a general feeling of communal celebration.

Univ of Texas Area

DATE	Last Saturday in April (rain date is the following Saturday)
TIME	Children's Area typically runs 11AM – 4PM; party ends at dark
LOCATION	Pease Park, 1100 Kingsbury St.
PARKING	Parking in the nearby neighborhoods fills up quickly so get there early or consider walking, biking or taking a shuttle. See website for shuttle locations.
WEBSITE	www.eeyores.com
ADMISSION	Free

Shakespeare in the Park

Each year, the Austin Shakespeare theater troupe performs one of the bard's plays in ***Zilker Park*** for the month of May. The productions are wonderful and typically provide a modern twist on the works. It's a great way to expose children to Shakespeare, as audiences watch from the grassy hillside. While the Shakespearean language might pose a challenge for keeping the attention of the youngest ones, energetic children can always roam the hill (glow sticks add to the excitement of the night and make it easier to keep up with them) or sleepy kids can relax on a blanket and stargaze while listening to the poetry of the language. Arrive early to set up a blanket close to the stage. Bring a cooler with drinks and dinner too, or grab snacks at the concession stand.

Zp
Zilker Park

DATES	Thursdays through Sundays in May
TIME	Performances begin at 8PM
LOCATION	2206 William Barton Dr., Beverly S. Sheffield Zilker Hillside Theater in Zilker Park (across from Barton Springs Pool)
WEBSITE	www.austinshakespeare.org
PHONE	(512) 470-4505
ADMISSION	Free, donations accepted. Metered parking is charged on weekends.

Nature Nights at Lady Bird Johnson Wildflower Center

Nature Nights are a series of educational events held during the summer at the ***Lady Bird Johnson Wildflower Center***. They are dedicated to teaching children about a particular aspect of Texas ecology, plants, or animals—from butterflies, bees, and frogs to birds of prey, snakes, and fossils. The Center is a beautiful place to spend the evening as kids learn through hands-on activities, crafts, expert-led hikes or hunts, musical guests, and activities related to the specific topic. A well-organized program that is lots of fun, kids have the run of the place on these nights, but their grown-ups might just learn something new too. Check the schedule for the weekly themes.

South Austin

DATES	Held on Thursday evenings during June—see online schedule for specific dates and topics
TIME	6PM – 9PM
LOCATION	Lady Bird Johnson Wildflower Center, 4801 La Cross Ave.
WEBSITE	www.wildflower.org/event/nature-nights
PHONE	(512) 232-0100
ADMISSION	Free

Austin Symphony Orchestra's Tuneful Tales

You can spot these summertime concerts happening from blocks away. Just follow the line of strollers, toddlers, and young children making their way towards the downtown Central Library. This two-hour, musical event series fills several stories of the library with interactive activities to introduce kids to classical music. Organized by the Austin Symphony Orchestra, participants can visit an instrument petting zoo and try out a variety of sounds with professional musicians. At another station, you can make your own instrument. Near the children's section on the third floor, you're in for a treat. The Austin Symphony Orchestra performs, filling the entire library with classical music aimed at a young audience. Check the online schedule for weekly topics. Due to the popularity of this annual family-friendly event and its downtown location, it's best to arrive early to find parking.

Downtown Austin

DATES Wednesday mornings in June and July

TIME 10:30AM – noon

LOCATION Central Library at 710 W. Cesar Chavez St.

PARKING See www.library.austintexas.gov/central/parking

WEBSITE www.austinsymphony.org/education-community/aso-tuneful-tales

ADMISSION Free

Beverly S. Sheffield Zilker Hillside Theater

Theater patrons of all ages spread their blankets on the grassy hillside on warm summer nights to watch Broadway musicals and Shakespeare under the stars. It's a wonderful, magical way to introduce children to theater in a relaxed setting. Go early (anytime after 6 PM) to secure a good spot, then let the kids roam the hill and explore. Or pack a picnic to enjoy at sunset as you watch the show. Snacks and drinks can also be purchased from the concession stand. The performances begin at dusk and run rather late, so bring a pillow and blanket for the young ones as they drift to sleep to some of the best bedtime stories ever.

Zp Zilker Park

DATES	Shakespeare in May; Musical from July – August
TIME	Dusk (approximately 8 PM)
LOCATION	2206 William Barton Dr. in Zilker Park across from Barton Springs Pool
WEBSITE	www.zilker.org/hillside
PHONE	(512) 479-9491
ADMISSION	Free, donations accepted. Metered parking is charged on weeekends.

Austin Museum Day

Austin Museum Day features free admission to dozens of participating museums with special events planned all day. It poses the perfect opportunity to pop into all of those you have been wanting to visit and do a museum tour of Austin. Or head to your favorite one to see what exciting activities or new exhibits have been added for the day. Check the website for locations and a schedule of events.

Multiple Locations

DATE Sunday in September

TIME All day

LOCATION Various museums throughout Austin (see website for listings)

WEBSITE www.austinmuseums.org

ADMISSION Free

Touch-A-Truck

You know you have arrived when you hear the sounds of horns blasting from eighteen-wheelers on Camp Mabry's airfield. Surrounded by a permanent exhibit of airplanes that line a large running track, trucks of all types fill the center of the field. Guests can sneak a peek inside a news van, hop aboard a school bus, and watch a cement truck whirl into action. Kids enamored with trucks will love climbing into the driver's seat of dump trucks, moving trucks, mail trucks, trash trucks, and tow trucks. When you get hungry, pop by a food truck and have a picnic under the trees. Across the street, you can also visit the Texas Military Forces Museum and the tanks along Armour Row.

Additionally, the event includes live music and kid activities, from a petting zoo and face painting to crafts and bouncy houses. Purchase a V.I.P. pass for early access and breakfast, or reserve a tent for a birthday party. Event sales support the Austin SAFE Alliance.

Because ***Camp Mabry*** is a military training camp, be prepared to show your I.D. to pass through the entrance checkpoint (further adding to the mystique of the event for young ones).

West Austin

DATE Saturday in September

TIME All day

LOCATION Camp Mabry, 3038 W. 35th St.

WEBSITE www.safeaustin.org/touchatruck

ADMISSION Free children 2 and under
$5 child ticket
$10 adults ticket

Austin City Limits Festival

The Austin City Limits Festival spans two weekends and showcases over one hundred bands, bringing local musicians and big acts from across the globe to play on its eight stages. The event is iconically Austin — not just in its support of live music but also with its high-tech scheduling features for the savvy festivalgoer, its green initiatives that include seas of bike racks and refillable water bottle stations, and its local food court populated by many of the city's favorite restaurants and craft beer makers.

Unlike many concerts, this one caters to kids too. The Austin Kiddie Limits stage features rocking kids' music and fun-filled activities. So this younger fan base can get decked out for fun shows with colored hair spray and tattoos, dance like crazy, and then take in the sand pile or the art and music activities between acts. Children age ten and under get into the festival free with a paying adult, and the kids' stage goes until the evening.

Tips if you plan to take the kids:

Be prepared!

Take sunblock, hats, refillable water bottles, earplugs or sound headphones for the kids, blankets, and blanket activities (a good book, drawing pads, balls, or games) plus walkie-talkies for older children (since cell service is often overloaded and unreliable at the festival). Enter the festival through the Family Entrance and make your first stop the Tag-a-Kid tent.

Set realistic expectations.

Plot out your ideal lineup, then be flexible. If you're taking the kids, realize that how much music you see will likely depend on your children's ages, endurance, and attention spans. Some parents get the three-day pass so they can come and go with the family and catch a couple of their favorite bands each day. Others set up camp at the kids' stage or manage a balance between family and adult shows with the help of a babysitter.

Plan your trip.

You can expect plenty of traffic and road closures as you near Zilker Park, so it's best to consider alternate modes of transportation. Check the "Getting There" section of the ACL Music Festival website for nearby parking garages and free shuttle information. Bike racks are also plentiful, and ride shares and pedicabs line nearby streets offering lifts to the festival gates.

Leave early.

Austin Kiddie Limits is a great spot for kids, but its lineup ends at 6 PM. This is a good time to exit before crowds surge for the night's closing acts.

Zp
Zilker Park

DATES	Two consecutive weekends in early October
TIME	10AM – 10PM
LOCATION	Zilker Park, 2100 Barton Springs Rd.
WEBSITE	www.aclfestival.com
ADMISSION	Single-day and three-day passes are available. Purchase these early through the website as the event often sells out.

Boo at the Zoo

Every October, the Austin Zoo hosts Boo at the Zoo on weekend evenings for their annual fundraiser. Wear a costume, pack a flashlight or glow stick, and experience the zoo at night! Halloween lights and decorations illuminate walkways so visitors can see the nocturnal animals that wake for the event. A Haunted Mansion with varied levels of spookiness adds thrill to the experience, or hop on the Haunted Train ride that runs every twenty minutes. For an additional fee, animal-themed kid shows entertain younger audiences. Picnic tables are available if you want to bring dinner or snacks.

West of Town

DATES Friday and Saturday nights in October

TIME Typically 6:30PM – 9PM

LOCATION 10808 Rawhide Trl.
The Zoo is located off of Hwy. 290 W. approximately 25 miles from downtown Austin and 2 1/2 miles from the "Y" at Oak Hill. To get there, take I-35 or Mopac Expy./Loop 1 to Hwy. 290 W. Turn right at the stoplight at Circle Dr. Follow it for 1½ miles. Turn right on Rawhide Trl. and follow the signs to the zoo.

WEBSITE www.austinzoo.org/boo-at-the-zoo

PHONE (512) 288-1490

ADMISSION $17.50 ages 2 and up
Ticket includes admission to the zoo, train ride, and unlimited Haunted House trips; shows cost extra for ages 2 and up. Seats for the train and entertainment are limited, so call ahead to reserve your spots! Advance tickets go on sale in early fall.

Crowe's Nest Farm Fall Family Fun Fest

See Crowe's Nest Farm entry under the "Places to Go" section

East of Town

DATES Weekends in October

LOCATION 10300 Taylor Ln., Manor

WEBSITE www.crowesnestfarm.org

PHONE (512) 272-4418

HOURS & ADMISSION Call for event times and admission prices.

Día de los Muertos Viva La Vida Fest

Hosted by Mexic-Arte Museum, this annual cultural festival honors the memories of loved ones through a lively, grand celebration of life in the Latin American tradition. An impressive Grand Procession takes the event from East Austin through downtown with a vibrant parade of giant puppets, props, floats, performers, and costumed participants. Crowds line the route to watch this colorful and eclectic mix of art, music, culture, and community in true Austin style. Fun, educational family activities and live entertainment follow. Through interactive, hands-on projects, kids can learn more about the Day of the Dead traditions. With Mexican and Tex-Mex food vendors, performances, and live music, the festival continues in all its vitality into the evening hours.

Downtown Austin

DATE Typically one of the last two weekends in October or the first weekend in November

TIME & LOCATION Check the website for event schedule and locations. Parade typically begins east of I-35 and moves the event into downtown Austin.

WEBSITE www.mexic-artemuseum.org

PHONE (512) 480-9373

ADMISSION Free

Texas Book Festival

Riding into town each November, authors, illustrators, publishers, booksellers, and bibliophiles of all ages take over the ***Texas State Capitol***. They line up tents of books along its grounds and fill its chambers with readings, book signings, author panels, storytimes, food, children's entertainment, and live music. Recognizing an avid readership (or at the very least, devoted picture book fans) among younger types with unbridled curiosity and shorter attention spans, there are plenty of activities to keep kids engaged in the Children's Read Me a Story Tent, Children's Activity Tent, and Children's Entertainment Tent. The book selections for kids are as wide ranging as the acts, which in years past have included puppets, magic shows, drawing lessons, and science experiments. Young adult readers can browse the latest titles or attend talks by some of their favorite authors. (Check the schedule of events for activities and times.) The festival location also provides the perfect opportunity to tour the Capitol or have a picnic on the open lawn while taking in the scene in celebration of books.

Downtown Austin

DATE	Weekend in November
TIME	Typically 10AM–5PM (although Lit Crawl for grown-ups runs much later)
LOCATION	Texas State Capitol (1100 Congress Ave.) and nearby venues (check schedule)
PARKING	Curbside metered parking is available on nearby streets (free on Sundays). Parking is also available in several state lots and in the Capitol Visitors Parking Garage with entrances on 12th and 13th Sts. between Trinity St. and San Jacinto Blvd. (See festival website for parking map.)
WEBSITE	www.texasbookfestival.org
PHONE	(512) 477-4055
ADMISSION	Free

Waterloo Greenway Creek Show

For a number of nights each November, guests stroll along Waller Creek for an outdoor art exhibit that highlights the beauty of the waterway through light. Artists, landscape architects, and designers stage glowing pieces along a stretch of the creek that will intrigue and delight. The experience takes about 20-30 minutes to walk through and ends at Waterloo Greenway Park. With the Texas State Capitol lit up in the distance, it's a beautiful way to spend a fall night in Austin.

At the park, you can grab a bite to eat and catch live music at the Moody Amphitheater with plenty of space to play, dance, and relax in the beer garden and on the lawn. Check the online schedule for the list of nightly activities and performances.

Downtown Austin

DATES	Nearly two weeks in November
TIME	6PM – 10PM
LOCATION	Along Waller Creek, ending at Waterloo Greenway
ADMISSION	Free $10 fast pass

Be prepared for a walk to the event entrance and for fairly long lines. They tend to be longest at opening and on weekends, when families are most likely to attend. The event is free, and walk-ups are welcome. It's best to go online and secure a reservation since some nights sell out once capacity is reached. Fast passes will get you in quicker and are available for a fee, with funds benefiting the Waterloo Greenway project.

Annual Events

Holiday Sing-Along and Downtown Stroll

For a wonderful event to begin the holiday season, grab your homemade sleds and head over to the Capitol for the annual tree lighting ceremony. Who says you can't have winter fun in Texas without snow? Kids spill over the rolling landscape of the Capitol grounds on cardboard sleds as crowds gather at the footsteps of the building to sing Christmas carols. At the appointed hour, everyone awaits the lighting of the forty-foot Christmas tree at the south gate. Festivities then continue along Congress Avenue to the Second Street District where retailers, cultural centers, and museums open their doors for extended hours and special events. Or enjoy live music as you shop the Holiday Market with tents filled with goods made by local artisans and food vendors. Check the website for the full schedule, including kid activities.

Downtown Austin

DATE	First Saturday in December
TIME	Typically 5PM – 10PM
LOCATION	1100 N. Congress Ave.
WEBSITE	www.downtownholidaystroll.com
PHONE	(512) 469-1766
ADMISSION	Free

Austin Trail of Lights

An Austin tradition, the Trail of Lights Festival attracts 400,000 annual visitors to Zilker Park during its two-week display. The park becomes aglow with tunnels of colored bulbs, decorated trees, and dozens of classic and contemporary holiday scenes stretching the 1.25 miles of stroller-friendly walking trail. Midway through the trail, stop for concessions, carnival rides, and local live music. The Trail of Lights Foundation also hosts sneak peeks, fun runs, and movie nights as well as ZiP Fast Passes that allow access the hour before the trail officially opens. While you're there, be sure to visit the ***Zilker Holiday Tree*** across the street. Turnout is heavy for this popular event, so go early and expect crowds.

Zp Zilker Park

DATES Two weeks during the Christmas holidays

TIME 7PM–10PM
ZiP Passes allow access one hour earlier.

LOCATION 2100 Barton Springs Rd.

PARKING Limited parking is available in the park with a prepaid parking pass, available online. (Be sure to note road closures during the Trail of Lights.) Off-site shuttles also run most nights from several locations around town for a minimal fee.

WEBSITES www.austintrailoflights.org

ADMISSION Free on some nights (see online calendar). For nights with an entrance fee, go online to purchase $5 gate entry and optional shuttle tickets, parking passes, ZiP Fast Passes, and/or platinum passes: www.austintrailoflights.org/tickets

Zilker Holiday Tree

Since 1967, Austinites of all ages have been dizzily whirling in circles under this 155-foot "tree" of lights. Strings of colorful bulbs spiral down from one of Austin's original Moon Towers that illuminated the city back in the late 1800's. Topped by a 150-bulb star, it's quite an impressive sight. The Zilker Tree is traditionally lit from the first Sunday in December through the end of the year. (You might consider combining this outing with the ***Austin Trail of Lights***.)

Zp
Zilker Park

DATE Check website for the date and time of the official Tree Lighting ceremony. The Zilker Tree stays lit at nights until January 1st.

TIME 6PM – 10PM

LOCATION 2201 Barton Springs Dr.

PARKING Limited paid parking is available in the park as well as off-site shuttles from several locations around town for a minimal fee. Be sure to note road closures during this time.

WEBSITE www.austintexas.gov/department/zilker-holiday-tree

ADMISSION Free

Luminations at the Lady Bird Johnson Wildflower Center

The ***Lady Bird Johnson Wildflower Center*** softly glows with thousands of luminarias and twinkling lights for this annual holiday event. Bring glow sticks or small flashlights and climb the Observation Tower for a beautiful view of the grounds from above. Local performers play live music on the grounds throughout the evening. Check the calendar for other special events as well. Kids can head to the Children's Garden or to the Little House for Christmas nature crafts and children's activities. Hot chocolate and goodies are available too, or make your own holiday dessert at the S'mores Bar where a few bucks grants access to a toasty fire and the makings for a holiday treat loaded with marshmallows and chocolates. It's a fun, festive way to begin the holiday season.

South Austin

DATE	Early/mid-December weekend
TIME	6PM – 9PM
LOCATION	4801 La Crosse Ave.
WEBSITE	www.wildflower.org/events
PHONE	(512) 232-0100
ADMISSION	Free children 4 and under $15 ages 5 and above

Christmas Lights on 37th Street

If you're on the lookout for uniquely festive Christmas lights, bundle up the kids, grab some hot chocolate, and head to 37th Street. You never know what you'll find amidst this eclectic mix of funky, historic bungalows, but you can be sure it will be quintessentially Austin. Just north of the University of Texas campus, this block goes all out, with lights stretching communally across the street from rooftop to rooftop, houses wrapped (literally) in a brilliant glow, and yards filled with creative scenes from sock monkey nativities to political satires to giant metal dinosaurs and stuffed animal petting zoos—all covered in lights. You're likely to come across residents playing live Christmas music in their front yards or greeting the stream of thousands of holiday goers who pass by each season. Park the car and walk so you can take in the scenes on both sides of the block, and even wander into welcoming backyards lit for the occasion.

North Central

DATES Typically mid-December through Christmas

LOCATION The block of 37th St. east of Guadalupe St. Traffic is one-way onto 37th St. and often backs up for the event. Consider parking on a nearby street and walking.

ADMISSION Free

Additional Resources

Book Website: www.ExploringAustinwithKids.com

Austin is a dynamic and rapidly growing city with no shortage of fun to be had. The website will keep you up-to-date with new places to explore, upcoming events, and day trips. You'll also find insider tips, interviews, and relevant ramblings about raising kids in the unique environs of Austin.

Family-Friendly Event Calendars

These websites are a great source of information on current kid events:

Do512Family blog and calendar keeps readers updated on kid-related happenings going on in and around Austin.
www.do512family.com

Austin Moms blog covers a range of parenting topics and has a weekly newsletter to keep you in the know about local family-friendly events.
www.austinmoms.com

Round the Rock covers local businesses, happenings, and special deals in neighboring Round Rock—a great resource for venturing north.
www.roundtherocktx.com

These print publications pinpoint children's events too and can be picked up at many local grocery stores, or you can find them online:

Austin Chronicle lists weekly kid events in the Community Calendar section.
www.austinchronicle.com/events/community/kids

Austin Family Magazine includes articles on parenting and a monthly calendar of family events and storytimes.
www.austinfamily.com

Community Impact Newspaper will keep you up to date with openings and closings of Austin area businesses and oftentimes lists a handful of family-friendly events in the monthly calendar.
www.communityimpact.com

Surrounding Areas & Day Trips

Whether you live just outside the city limits or are looking for nearby day trips, these places are well worth checking out. (See the guide for entries with an asterisk.)

NORTH

Georgetown

All Things Kid
Blue Hole
Lake Georgetown
Inner Space Caverns

Leander

Quarry Splash Pad
Cedar Rock Railroad

Pflugerville

Northeast Metropolitan Park BMX Track and Skate Park

Round Rock

Brushy Creek Trail
Prete Main Street Plaza
Play for All Park*
Rock 'N River Water Park
Round Rock Donuts
Round Rock Express*

SOUTH

San Marcos

Meadows Center
Wonder World

New Braunfels

Landa Park
McKenna Children's Museum
Schlitterbahn

Wimberley

Blue Hole Regional Park
Emily Ann Theatre
Jacob's Well Natural Area
Wimberley Glassworks
Wimberley Market Days

EAST

Bastrop

Bastrop State Park
Buescher State Park

Cedar Creek

Dinosaur Park*
McKinney Roughs*

WEST

Bee Caves

Bee Cave Sculpture Park
Hill Country Galleria

Dripping Springs

Hamilton Pool*
Pedernales Falls State Park*

Johnson City & Stonewall

Exotic Resort Zoo
Hill Country Science Mill
Sauer-Beckmann Living History Farm

Marble Falls

Sweet Berry Farm

Spicewood

Krause Springs*

Acknowledgments

I am indebted to the many parents, grandparents, friends, and family members whose insights, tips, sharing of secret spots, photographs, and feedback every step of the way has led to this book. You continue to improve this guide. Thank you for your ongoing, wholehearted support!

Over the past few years, I feel fortunate to have met so many local shop owners, buyers, managers, and program directors whose passion, friendliness, and pure joy are such an inspiration. You are what makes Austin the place we love.

Wordsmiths Jodi Egerton, Laurie Filipelli, and Carol Kim, for your finesse in editing new material and for not letting me skimp on the details, readers thank you. I was excited to collaborate with Monica Thomas once again, who has made the content in this updated edition even more accessible through her creative, thoughtful approach to book design, and thanks to Tamara Dever of TLC Graphics for her patience, warmth, and professionalism. It is an honor to work with such a team.

Deborah Lykins did amazing work in designing the website for the book. She not only shared photographs for the project, she and her husband Ben also shared their youngest child for unforgettable Friday adventures.

A sincere thanks goes to my homebody son, Stone, for leaving the house so many times and packing a healthy skepticism about our adventures that led to insightful and, admittedly, fun outings. He constantly reminds me to slow down and enjoy the simple pleasures. Thank you to my oldest, Andrew, whose positive outlook and thirst for adventure I can always count on for fun expeditions. I appreciate his honest insights, editing tips, and readiness to contribute art for the cause. Finally, I am grateful to my husband Daniel for his listening ear as I made him play the role of a tourist in Austin while I read entries aloud and for his unflagging encouragement and support in all ways.

You all fill Austin with so many great memories at every turn!

Photo Credits

Photographs by Jamie Allen:
AISD playgrounds, Barton Creek Greenbelt, Rodeo Austin

Photographs by Jessica Attie:
Barton Springs Pool, Boggy Creek Farm sunflowers, BookPeople, Dougherty Arts, Hamilton Pool, Mayfield Park

Photograph by Nicole Basham: Texas Memorial Museum

Photograph by Adriana Cantu: Zilker Park Playscape

Photographs by Carissa DeAngelis and courtesy of Kristen Baucher:
Austin Zoo, Pedernales River at Reimers Ranch

Photograph by Paige Deshong: Peter Pan Mini-Golf

Photograph courtesy of Heather O'Keeffe Gardner: Playland Skate Center

Photograph by Erin Geisler: Holiday Sing-Along and Downtown Stroll

Photograph by Devon Hutchins, courtesy of Pease Park Conservancy:
Squirrel Fest

Photographs by Kelly Lynn James, courtesy of the Blanton Museum of Art:
Blanton Museum of Art

Photographs by Deborah Lykins: Alamo Drafthouse, Splash! Exhibit

Photograph by Liz McGuire: Austin City Limits Festival

Photographs by April Moore: Central Market, City of Austin Splash Pads

Photograph by Pinkle Toes Photography: Big Top Candy Shop

Photograph by Natalie Poulos: City of Austin Parks

Photograph by Ashley Thompson: Irving and Hazeline Smith Trail

Index

About the Author

Local author Annette Lucksinger has made her home in Austin, Texas, for the past twenty-five years. She is a mother of two children, who not only inspired the guidebook but who have proven to be great fellow adventurers. She spends her summers at Camp Longhorn where she works as Merit Store Director alongside her family. Her favorite place to be is outside with kids.

CPSIA information can be obtained
at www.ICGtesting.com
Printed in the USA
BVHW040938060423
661869BV00016B/990

9 780991 227044